NO MINOR MATTER
Children in Maryland's Jails

Human Rights Watch

New York • Washington • London • Brussels

Printed in the United States of America

ISBN: 1-56432-243-2
Library of Congress Catalog Card Number: 99-067865

 Baltimore City Detention Center.

Cover design by Rafael Jiménez

Addresses for Human Rights Watch
350 Fifth Avenue, 34th Floor, New York, NY 10118-3299
Tel: (212) 290-4700, Fax: (212) 736-1300, E-mail: hrwnyc@hrw.org

1630 Connecticut Avenue, N.W., Suite 500, Washington, DC 20009
Tel: (202) 612-4321, Fax: (202) 612-4333, E-mail: hrwdc@hrw.org

33 Islington High Street, N1 9LH London, UK
Tel: (171) 713-1995, Fax: (171) 713-1800, E-mail: hrwatchuk@gn.apc.org

15 Rue Van Campenhout, 1000 Brussels, Belgium
Tel: (2) 732-2009, Fax: (2) 732-0471, E-mail:hrwatcheu@skynet.be

Web Site Address: http://www.hrw.org

Listserv address: To subscribe to the list, send an e-mail message to majordomo@igc.apc.org with "subscribe hrw-news" in the body of the message (leave the subject line blank).

Human Rights Watch is dedicated to
protecting the human rights of people around the world.

We stand with victims and activists to prevent
discrimination, to uphold political freedom, to protect people from inhumane
conduct in wartime, and to bring offenders to justice.

We investigate and expose
human rights violations and hold abusers accountable.

We challenge governments and those who hold power to end abusive practices
and respect international human rights law.

We enlist the public and the international
community to support the cause of human rights for all.

HUMAN RIGHTS WATCH

Human Rights Watch conducts regular, systematic investigations of human rights abuses in some seventy countries around the world. Our reputation for timely, reliable disclosures has made us an essential source of information for those concerned with human rights. We address the human rights practices of governments of all political stripes, of all geopolitical alignments, and of all ethnic and religious persuasions. Human Rights Watch defends freedom of thought and expression, due process and equal protection of the law, and a vigorous civil society; we document and denounce murders, disappearances, torture, arbitrary imprisonment, discrimination, and other abuses of internationally recognized human rights. Our goal is to hold governments accountable if they transgress the rights of their people.

Human Rights Watch began in 1978 with the founding of its Europe and Central Asia division (then known as Helsinki Watch). Today, it also includes divisions covering Africa, the Americas, Asia, and the Middle East. In addition, it includes three thematic divisions on arms, children's rights, and women's rights. It maintains offices in New York, Washington, Los Angeles, London, Brussels, Moscow, Dushanbe, Rio de Janeiro, and Hong Kong. Human Rights Watch is an independent, nongovernmental organization, supported by contributions from private individuals and foundations worldwide. It accepts no government funds, directly or indirectly.

The staff includes Kenneth Roth, executive director; Michele Alexander, development director; Reed Brody, advocacy director; Carroll Bogert, communications director; Barbara Guglielmo, finance director; Jeri Laber special advisor; Lotte Leicht, Brussels office director; Patrick Minges, publications director; Susan Osnos, associate director; Maria Pignataro Nielsen, human resources director; Jemera Rone, counsel; Wilder Tayler, general counsel; and Joanna Weschler, United Nations representative. Jonathan Fanton is the chair of the board. Robert L. Bernstein is the founding chair.

The regional directors of Human Rights Watch are Peter Takirambudde, Africa; José Miguel Vivanco, Americas; Sidney Jones, Asia; Holly Cartner, Europe and Central Asia; and Hanny Megally, Middle East and North Africa. The thematic division directors are Joost R. Hiltermann, arms; Lois Whitman, children's rights; and Regan Ralph, women's rights.

ACKNOWLEDGMENTS

This report was written by Michael Bochenek, counsel to the Children's Rights Division of Human Rights Watch, based on information that the author and Jo Becker, advocacy director of the Children's Rights Division, gathered during visits to five Maryland jails from July 1998 to May 1999. Mark Soler, a member of the Children's Rights Division's advisory committee and the president of the Youth Law Center, and Dr. Andrea Weisman, director of mental health services for the court-appointed receiver for medical and mental health services at the Central Detention Facility, Washington, D.C., were part of the Human Rights Watch delegation that toured the Baltimore City Detention Center in May 1999 and contributed to the sections on discipline, medical and mental health services, and education. Lois Whitman, executive director of the Children Rights Division, and Cynthia Brown, program director of Human Rights Watch, edited the report. Jo Becker; Widney Brown, advocacy coordinator of the Women's Rights Division; Allyson Collins, senior researcher; Jamie Fellner, associate counsel; Joe Saunders, associate counsel; Mark Soler; Wilder Tayler, general counsel; and Andrea Weisman reviewed and commented on the manuscript. Fitzroy Hepkins, Patrick Minges, and Shalu Rozario provided production assistance.

We wish to express our deep appreciation to the children who spoke with us and to the many lawyers, judges, academics, government officials, and juvenile rights advocates who assisted us with our research. The names of all of the children we interviewed have been changed to protect their privacy.

We thank the members of the Children's Rights Division's advisory committee and the many other individuals who provided helpful suggestions and assistance during the course of our investigation. In particular, Mark Soler; Robert Schwartz, executive director of the Juvenile Law Center; and Andrea Weisman made invaluable contributions to this report. We are also grateful for the help of Shirley D. Brandman, Esq.; Shawn Brune, Advocates for Families and Youth; Marianna Burt, Esq.; Professor Doug Colbert, University of Maryland School of Law; Sarah Cushman, community organizer, American Civil Liberties Union of Maryland–Eastern Shore; Monique Dixon, staff attorney, Public Justice Center; Frank Dunbaugh, Esq.; Heather Ford, Advocates for Families and Youth; M. Cristina Gutierrez, Esq.; Professor Susan Leviton, University of Maryland School of Law; Bart Lubow, senior associate, The Annie E. Casey Foundation; James Paul McComb, executive director, Maryland Association of Resources for Family and Youth; Mark B. Martin, Esq.; Diane Paul, consultant, Human Rights Watch; Patricia Puritz, consultant, Juvenile Justice Center, American Bar Association Criminal Justice Section; Stephen Sachs, Esq.; Marc Schindler, staff attorney, Youth Law Center; Dr. Deborah Shelton, assistant professor, University of Maryland School of Nursing; Stuart O. Simms, secretary, Maryland Department of Public Safety and Correctional Services; Josef Szwarc, researcher, Americas

Regional Program, Amnesty International; Deborah H. Thompson, senior staff attorney, Public Justice Center; the Honorable Martin P. Welch, chief judge, Circuit Court for Baltimore City; Leval Wilson, staff attorney, Juvenile Law Center; and the Honorable David W. Young, judge, Circuit Court for Baltimore City. In addition, we thank the individuals who asked that their names not be mentioned.

We also wish to express our thanks to the directors and staff of the Baltimore City Detention Center, the Frederick County Detention Center, the Mongomery County Department of Correction and Rehabilitation, the Prince George's County Department of Corrections, and the Washington County Detention Center for facilitating our access to the facilities we visited and for responding cordially and responsively to our numerous queries and requests.

Grants from the Abell Foundation and The Annie E. Casey Foundation made this investigation possible.

TABLE OF CONTENTS

I. SUMMARY AND RECOMMENDATIONS

With frequent references to "juvenile predators," "hardened criminals," and "young thugs," U.S. lawmakers at both the state and federal levels have increasingly abandoned efforts to rehabilitate child offenders through the juvenile court system. Instead, many states have responded to a perceived outbreak in juvenile violent crime by moving more children into the adult criminal system. Between 1992 and 1998, at least forty U.S. states adopted legislation making it easier for children to be tried as adults; a similar measure for youth charged with federal crimes is pending in the U.S. Congress. These measures neither reduce crime nor lead to rehabilitation. But they often do lead to serious abuses when children are held in adult jails, sometimes in appalling conditions of confinement, occasionally sharing cells with adult detainees, and frequently provided inadequate education, medical and mental health care, or age-appropriate recreational opportunities.

Joey N., seventeen, had spent over six months in the Baltimore City Detention Center when he was interviewed by Human Rights Watch in March 1999. "This jail's crazy," he told us. During his first three months in the detention center, when he was in the juvenile general population section, he regularly saw juvenile detainees carrying weapons. "The whole section has knives," he told us. "People got to keep them for a reason, because they fear for their life." On several occasions, all of the youth in the section were restricted to their cells for extended periods of time after fights broke out between several youth. During one such period, he reported, "C.O.'s [correction officers] came, took everything we had. Sheets, everything. They left us in the cells for two days with no clothing except for our boxers. All the windows were open. I got sick real bad. This was when it was snowing, and we didn't have no heat. We didn't have no t-shirts or blankets or nothing. It was freezing cold."

When Joey N. was placed in disciplinary segregation in January 1999, the adult detainees in the section continually harassed him by throwing excrement and urine into his cell. "I complained to the C.O.'s, but they didn't do nothing," he said. In desperation, he resorted to telling the guards that he was suicidal, and he was moved to the psychiatric wing for several days. On his return to the segregation section, he asked the guards to place him in one of the section's isolation cells. Heavy metal sheets completely cover the bars, preventing other detainees in the section from throwing feces into the cell but also blocking all natural light. Joey N. told us, "I asked to go in this cell, they call it the dungeon. Dungeon's the one got a steel door. Ain't nothing in it, just a toilet and a bed. I'm the only person in there. I stay there twenty-four hours a day, only come out

Tuesday and Friday for a five-minute shower, then get locked back in." (In this report, all names of youth have been changed to protect their privacy.)

The national movement to charge more youth in the adult criminal system is premised on the inaccurate assumptions that juvenile crime is on the rise and that trying children as adults will reduce crime. In fact, juvenile crime has declined steadily even as the proponents of harsh juvenile sentencing have predicted an onslaught of adolescent offenders. In addition, studies in at least five states have concluded that laws that make it easier to transfer children to adult courts do not measurably reduce violent crime.

Minority children—African-American youth in particular—are disproportionately sent to criminal court under these policies. In Maryland, cases involving black youth represent seven out of every ten cases in which the juvenile judge orders a transfer to criminal court, even though less than one-third of the state's population is African-American.

Lost in the zeal to get tough on adolescent offenders is the fact that they are still children. Once placed in the adult system, youth often lose the opportunity to participate in specialized programs designed to rehabilitate them. They may be placed in pretrial detention with adults, and if convicted they are held, for the most part, in adult correctional institutions. As one Maryland youth observed, "Being here with adults, that ain't going to rehabilitate me, it just teaching me to be a better criminal."

Once charged in the adult criminal system, many children are locked up in local jails, often for six months or more, while their cases are tried. In Maryland, between 200 and 300 children are in adult detention facilities on any given day. Imposing facilities designed to hold adults, jails often lack the infrastructure, the programs, and the staff to handle juveniles. "We're not trained to be babysitters," commented Barry Stanton, the director of the Prince George's County Correctional Center, in an interview with Human Rights Watch in July 1998. "Don't ask me to be a mental health expert, a teacher, a disciplinarian for juveniles. It's not my job."

Some 150 children, between one-half and two-thirds of all youth held in Maryland's jails, are in the Baltimore City Detention Center, a decaying facility nearly two hundred years old, where they endure appalling conditions of confinement. Children in Baltimore's jail spend their days in grim cells lacking direct natural lighting and crawling with cockroaches, rodents, and other vermin. Ineffective heating and poor ventilation offer little relief from the heat of the summer months and the chill of the winter.

In all jails, children face greater risks to their safety and well-being than do youth held in juvenile facilities. They are at risk of harm from other juveniles: lacking the space to classifly children who are admitted, many jails cannot separate potentially dangerous youth from those who are vulnerable. But incidents of violence regularly occur even when jails have made efforts at classification. In Montgomery County's Youthful Offender Unit, for example, a seventeen-year-old detainee told Human Rights Watch in July 1998 that fighting "happens every night. You can hear it, the sound of fists hitting raw skin."

Violence is particularly severe in the Baltimore City Detention Center, where the crumbling infrastructure gives inmates many opportunities to fashion handmade weapons, known as "shanks." In order to restrict the flow of weapons onto the juvenile section of the jail, guards thoroughly search children on their way to and from classes, usually subjecting them to a strip search as they return to the section.

Some of the Baltimore City Detention Center's guards permit fights between youth, a practice known as the "square dance." Children in the city's detention center report that some guards will ask if there are any youth who want to settle scores. If there are, guards will lock the remainder of the children in their cells; the fight takes place in an eight-foot-by-eight-foot square area on one of the tiers. "It ends up with busted heads, slashes over your eyes, broken fingers, cut lips, maybe a broken nose," a former juvenile detainee told Human Rights Watch in March 1999. "But you don't go to the hospital for the cuts. If you did, there'd have to be a report, and the guards would have to explain why two guys were out in the square while everybody else was locked in," he added.

Children also face risks from adult inmates, with whom they may have daily contact and may even share cells. Commingling is the norm in many of Maryland's smaller jails, including the detention centers in Frederick and Washington Counties. Even in the larger jails, which generally have separate juvenile housing sections, children regularly come into contact with adults when they take meals, use the gym, visit the doctor, or go to court. Moreover, the larger jails routinely house children with adults when they are placed in administrative segregation or other special housing.

Disciplinary practices in the Baltimore City Detention Center raise serious concerns of arbitrary and excessive punishment. We found that many children in Baltimore are given lengthy terms of confinement to cells in the disciplinary segregation section, often with loss of visits and other privileges, sometimes for relatively minor offenses. In serious cases, disciplinary hearing officers routinely order juveniles segregated for ninety days per charge, the maximum sanction possible. In some cases, the hearing officers direct juveniles to serve consecutive sanctions on multiple charges, resulting in periods of segregration of 180 days or more.

We also found that officials in the Baltimore City Detention Center frequently place the general population on extended cell confinement, called "lockdown," in response to escape attempts or fights. Children on lockdown may receive up to two or three showers each week and are usually permitted to attend classes; otherwise, they remain inside their cells and are not allowed visits from family members. Such measures often last for weeks after the incident that gave rise to them and continue long after the offenders are identified and disciplined. When lockdowns remain in effect beyond their immediate security purpose, they constitute collective punishments, a practice prohibited by international standards.

Further, Baltimore detention center officials enjoy broad latitude to place juveniles on administrative segregation the entire time they are in the jail. The decision to place a detainee in administrative segregation, which Baltimore officials call "supermax," is completely discretionary, based solely on the warden's review of the youth's record; detainees have no right to a hearing and no right to seek review of the warden's determination.

In general, children reported few problems with guards. Where we did hear of abuses by guards, the accounts suggested a common pattern of guards overreacting—sometimes violently—to teenage backtalk. These cases demonstrate that specialized training in adolescent developmental issues is critical for jail staff who work regularly with youth.

The education provided to children was seriously deficient. The most extreme case was the Prince George's County Correctional Center, which provided no schooling whatsoever to boys in detention, some thirty at the time of our July 1998 visit. In the other jails, we found that the number of hours of classroom instruction frequently fell far short of the requirements of federal and state law.

We were also disturbed to find serious deficiencies in the mental health program in the Baltimore City Detention Center, the only mental health program we were able to analyze in depth. Mental health services in Baltimore's jail are minimal to nonexistent, with no services specifically for juveniles. There are no therapeutic groups, no individual counseling, and no efforts at aftercare planning. In practice, the only inmates who are able to receive mental health services are those in crisis, who are housed in deplorable conditions. Touring the mental health unit, we saw inmates who were naked, with nothing more than paper blankets to cover their bodies; no medical necessity justified this dehumanizing practice.

The lack of appropriate mental health care is especially troubling because children in detention are more likely than youth as a whole to have mental health needs, and the conditions in which they are confined may well exacerbate their preexisting mental disabilities. Even for those youth who do not come to jail with prior mental health needs, being jailed takes an emotional toll. Indeed, research suggests that children in jails may be eight times more likely to commit suicide than their peers held in juvenile detention centers.

While every jail we visited offered basic medical services to detainees and examined them upon their arrival, we heard frequent complaints that sick children had to wait for several days or weeks before they were seen by medical staff. Some youth told us that their requests for assistance were ignored altogether. Our investigation left us with questions about the adequacy of basic medical care for female detainees in particular. We learned, for example, that the Washington County Detention Center did not routinely offer girls and women gynecological examinations, contrary to the recommendation of the National Commission on Correctional Health Care. In addition, we were troubled to find that not all jails separated men and women who were in need of observation for medical or mental health reasons.

Girls in adult detention facilities suffer particular hardships. Because of the small numbers of girls in detention, girls who are held separately from adults may spend hours of their day in virtual isolation.

Other aspects of jail life reinforced the conclusion that while some children, particularly those accused of committing violent offenses, may need to be detained in juvenile institutions pending trial, they do not belong in jail with adult inmates. The detention centers we visited may not offer youth enough exercise opportunity to meet their developmental needs. They offer few other activities for juveniles, placing children held in jails at a disadvantage to their peers in the juvenile detention system. Children placed on disciplinary segregation are frequently denied visits and phone calls for as long as ninety days or more, depriving them of contact with the wider community that can be crucial to their well-being. Finally, children in all jails complained that they did not get enough to eat. When we spoke with jail officials about the meal portions served to juveniles, it appeared that they had not taken the dietary needs of adolescents into account in providing meals.

Maryland's jails are inappropriate places for youth, even for those who are accused of committing very serious crimes. This conclusion is particularly compelling with regard to the Baltimore City Detention Center, where children endure dimly lit, dreary cells infested with vermin and face daily risks to their personal safety. Whether or not they are detained in conditions as squalid as those in the Baltimore, youth held in Maryland's adult detention centers receive insufficient opportunities for education and recreation and face protracted periods of idleness. They may not be afforded age-appropriate medical and mental health services, and it appeared that all jails failed to provide youth with enough food to meet their developmental needs.

Methodology

This report is one of a series of reports published by Human Rights Watch on the conditions of confinement for children. In the United States, we have investigated and reported on juvenile detention facilities in Colorado, Georgia, and Louisiana, and we have published two reports on detention conditions for unaccompanied minors in the custody of the U.S. Immigration and Naturalization Service. Elsewhere in the world, we have documented detention conditions of children in Bulgaria, Guatemala, India, Jamaica, Kenya, and Pakistan.

Prisons, jails, police lockups, and other places of detention pose special research problems because of their closed nature and because their inmates, especially those who are minors, are vulnerable to intimidation and retaliation. In the interests of accuracy and objectivity, Human Rights Watch bases its reporting on first-hand observation of detention conditions and direct interviews with prisoners and corrections officials, although we have devised an alternative research methodology for use when authorities bar access to outside monitoring. Human Rights Watch follows a set of self-imposed rules in conducting investigations: our investigators undertake visits only when we, not the authorities, can choose the institutions to be visited; when we can be confident that we will be allowed to talk privately with the detainees of their choice; and when we can gain access to the entire facility to be examined. These rules ensure that investigators are not shown "model" detention centers, "model" inmates, or the most presentable parts of the facilities under investigation. In the rare cases in which entry on these terms is denied, Human Rights Watch may conduct its investigations on the basis of interviews with former inmates, relatives of inmates, lawyers, prison experts, and detention center staff, as well as documentary evidence.

As we do when working with other vulnerable groups, we take particular care to ensure that interviews of children are confidential, conducted with sensitivity, and free from any actual or apparent outside influence. We do not print the names or other identifying information of the children in detention whom we interview. In this report, all children are given aliases to protect their privacy.

In this report as well as in all of our previous reports, we assess the treatment of children in the justice system according to the guidelines set forth in the United Nations Standard Minimum Rules for the Treatment of Prisoners, the Body of Principles for the Protection of All Persons under Any Form of Detention or Imprisonment, the United Nations Rules for the Protection of Juveniles Deprived of their Liberty, and the United Nations Standard Minimum Rules for the Administration of Juvenile Justice.

Access to Detention Centers

In the United States, Human Rights Watch researchers have generally been afforded access to the facilities we seek to investigate. Human Rights Watch received full access to seven state-operated juvenile institutions and one private contract facility in Colorado in 1996 and 1997 and was also accorded access to the four secure juvenile correctional facilities in Louisiana in 1995. In 1996 the Immigration and Naturalization Service granted our request for access to detention centers maintained in Los Angeles county and Arizona, and in 1998 the agency granted a similar request for access to a Pennsylvania county facility with which it contracts to house undocumented minors. We have also been able to conduct interviews and on-site investigations at adult prisons and jails in California, Colorado, Florida, Georgia, Illinois, Indiana, Michigan, Minnesota, New York, Oklahoma, Texas, and Virginia. In a significant exception to these commendably open practices, Georgia's Department of Children and Youth Services refused to permit Human Rights Watch to visit juvenile facilities or to conduct interviews with children in those facilities when we sought access in February 1996.

We requested access to seven pretrial detention facilities in Maryland: two in the Baltimore area, two in the Washington, D.C., area, two in western Maryland, and one on Maryland's Eastern Shore. Two jails—the Baltimore County Detention Center in Towson and the Wicomico County Detention Center, on the Eastern Shore—flatly refused to permit Human Rights Watch researchers to visit. The detention centers in Frederick County, Montgomery County, Prince George's County, and Washington County responded immediately to our requests for access, according us unrestricted access and permitting our researchers to conduct confidential interviews of children in detention. We received the full cooperation of jail officials at each of these facilities, and we found the staff at all facilities to be accessible, open, and helpful.

The Baltimore City Detention Center eventually granted us unconditional access to the facility and the juvenile inmates, but only after some ten months of negotiation. Detention center officials permitted us to visit the Baltimore City Detention Center in September 1998, three months after our initial request, but denied us access to all juvenile housing sections and refused to permit us to speak to youth in detention. After several additional months of negotiation and a meeting with Secretary of Public Safety and Correctional Services Stuart O. Simms, we reached an agreement that permitted us to visit the detention center under the terms we had originally proposed. When we visited the facility in May 1999, the commissioner and his staff gave us unrestricted access to every part of the jail we asked to see, allowed us to examine disciplinary reports and other records, and permitted us to speak privately with youth. The sole condition of our interviews was that representatives of Maryland's Office of the Public Defender (OPD) would be available at the detention center to answer any questions youth might have on their particular cases. The OPD representatives introduced themselves to each juvenile we had selected to interview but did not sit in on our interviews.

In total, we were able to interview some sixty children—ten in Prince George's County, seven in Montgomery County, four in Washington County, and the remainder in Baltimore. We conducted all interviews of children in private, out of sight and earshot of corrections officers and other jail officials. In addition to interviews with children and site visits, we inspected jail disciplinary reports, court records, and other records obtained through requests under Maryland's Public Information Act. We also spoke with local judges, children's rights advocates, defense attorneys, academics, and government officials.

Recommendations

To the Maryland General Assembly

- Strictly limit the practice of trying children in the criminal courts. There should be a presumption in favor of adjudicating children's cases in the juvenile justice system. The transfer of children's cases to the criminal court should be limited to extraordinarily severe cases.
- Repeal or modify existing transfer provisions that automatically require all children charged with certain offenses to be tried as adults. The decision to transfer a case to the criminal courts should be subject to judicial discretion; transfers should not be mandatory and should not be left to the discretion of the prosecutor.
- Take immediate steps to end the practice of placing children under the age of eighteen in adult detention facilities. Maryland's jails subject youth to the risk of violence and potentially abusive disciplinary practices, problems which are compounded by systemic deficiencies in staff training, insufficient opportunities for education and recreation, a lack of appropriate medical and mental health care, and a failure even to provide youth with enough to eat. In view of these abusive conditions, the time and expense that would be required to correct these violations individually, and the small numbers of youth held in Maryland's adult detention system, Human Rights Watch believes that the most expedient and safest course of action is to end the practice of detaining juveniles in adult jails.
- Until the practice of placing children in adult detention facilities is ended, correct the confinement of disproportionate numbers of minority children in adult jails.

To the Maryland Courts

- Order pretrial detention of juveniles only as a measure of last resort and for the shortest appropriate period of time.
- Ensure the shortest possible period of pretrial detention by expediting cases in which the juvenile defendant is detained.

To the Maryland Department of Public Safety and Correctional Services and to county jail administrations

Separation from Adult Inmates

- Children must be separated from adult inmates at all times.

Conditions of Confinement

- Ensure that the conditions of confinement for children meet all of the requirements of health, safety, and human dignity.
- Provide all children with food that is sufficient to meet their developmental needs.
- Both inside and outside their cells, permit children to wear ordinary clothing rather than stigmatizing, institutionalizing, and uncomfortable uniforms.
- Provide children with adequate mattresses and clean bedding, which should be changed often enough to ensure cleanliness and should be appropriate for the season.
- Allow children to shower every day.

Disciplinary Practices

- Prohibit the use of isolation as a disciplinary measure.
- Administrative segregation and protective custody should be used only where absolutely necessary for the protection of a child. Where such placement is necessary, it should be employed for the shortest possible period of time. A decision to place a child in administrative segregation should be promptly and systematically reviewed.
- Children in segregation should never be denied access to reading matter.
- Visits by parents, guardians, or other responsible adults should not be suspended for those children placed in segregation.
- Provide clear guidelines for hearing officers and detention center staff who impose discipline.
- Upon entry, all youth should receive a handbook that clearly specifies what behaviors are prohibited and what sanctions they may receive for each behavior.

- All youth should receive written and verbal explanations of the disciplinary process, including an explanation of their right to seek review of disciplinary actions.

Staff

- Provide all staff with specialized training for dealing with children and adolescents. All staff should be trained in and continually reminded of the importance of proper, respectful treatment of juveniles and other inmates. Abusive conduct by staff, including derogatory remarks, should not be tolerated.
- Ensure that jail staff protect children from assaults by other children. When such an assault occurs, staff should take appropriate measures to protect the child.

Education

- In accordance with state law and binding international obligations, ensure that every child below the age of sixteen receives an education suited to his or her needs and abilities and designed to prepare him or her for return to society.
- Ensure that all detainees sixteen years of age and older have the opportunity to continue their education if they wish to do so.
- In accordance with state and federal law, provide special education for all inmates who qualify to receive it.

Girls Detained in Adult Jails

- Girls in detention should receive care, protection, assistance, treatment, and training that is consistent with international standards. They should never receive less care, protection, assistance, treatment, or training than that given to boys in detention.

To the Maryland Commission on Correctional Standards, the American Correctional Association, and the National Commission on Correctional Health Care

- Review existing standards applicable to adult jails to ensure that they reflect the needs of youth who may be detained in facilities designed primarily for adults.

To the United States Congress

- Withdraw the restrictive reservations, declarations, and understandings that the United States has attached to the International Covenant on Civil and Political Rights.
- Introduce implementing legislation for the International Convention on Civil and Political Rights.
- Ratify the Convention on the Rights of the Child.
- Amend the Individuals with Disabilities Education Act to require states to report annually on the number of detained or incarcerated children with disabilities, by race, ethnicity, and disability category, who are receiving a free appropriate public education.

To the United States Department of Justice

- The Special Litigation Section of the U.S. Department of Justice's Civil Rights Division should investigate the conditions of confinement of children detained in Maryland's jails.

II. TRYING CHILDREN IN ADULT COURTS

When I first came to the court, everybody was talking about the "juvenile superpredators," so I kept waiting on the superpredators. They never came. I never saw any superpredators in my court. What I saw were fourteen- and fifteen-year-olds, scared to death.

—Judge David A. Young, Circuit Court for Baltimore City, June 5, 1998

With frequent references to "juvenile predators," "hardened criminals," and "young thugs," U.S. lawmakers at both the state and federal levels have increasingly abandoned efforts to rehabilitate child offenders through the juvenile court system. Instead, many states have responded to a perceived outbreak in juvenile violent crime by moving more children into the adult criminal system. Between 1992 and 1998, at least forty U.S. states adopted legislation making it easier for children to be tried as adults.[1]

Maryland's juvenile justice policy is indicative of this nationwide trend. In 1994, the state overhauled its juvenile justice system to exclude a large number of offenses from the jurisdiction of the juvenile courts, in effect making it easier to try a child as an adult,[2] and in 1997 the General Assembly approved a measure opening juvenile court hearings to the public when the child is charged with committing an offense that would be a felony if committed by an adult.[3]

In Maryland and elsewhere in the United States, the trial of children as adults often fails to provide children with the special safeguards and care to which they are entitled under international law. The decision to send children into the adult system has been criticized as arbitrary and unfair, with racial and ethnic minorities overrepresented among the juvenile population transferred to criminal court. Once in the adult system, youth are deprived of the wide variety of rehabilitative

---

[1]In this report, the word "children" refers to anyone under the age of eighteen. The Convention on the Rights of the Child defines as a child "every human being under the age of eighteen years unless, under the law applicable to the child, majority is attained earlier." Convention on the Rights of the Child, Article 1, G.A. Res. 44/25, U.N. Doc. A/RES/44/25 (adopted November 20, 1989; entered into force September 2, 1990).

[2]*See* David L. Addison, "Which Court: Juvenile or Criminal?," *Maryland Bar Journal,* November/December 1997, p. 32 (discussing the passage of House Bill 1122 in 1994 and subsequent technical amendments in 1995 and 1996). "As originally written, the bill would even have excluded individuals from age fourteen through seventeen charged with these offenses, but it was amended to apply only to sixteen- and seventeen-year-olds." Ibid.

[3]*See* Ivan Penn, "Juvenile Hearings Open Up," *The Sun*, October 2, 1997, p. 1A.

sentencing options that they might be eligible to receive in the juvenile court system—sentencing options that are designed to give them the tools they need to turn their lives around and become law-abiding members of society. A conviction in adult court leaves an adolescent with a lasting criminal record. Finally, as detailed in subsequent chapters of this report, youth charged as adults may be placed in pretrial detention in adult jails, often called "local detention centers," facilities which often lack the infrastructure, programs, or staff to handle juveniles.

The Myth of the "Superpredator"

Proponents of measures to try increasing numbers of juveniles as adults assert that violent crime by youth is on the upswing and project even higher levels of crime by violent juvenile offenders in the future. Often couching their arguments in extremist terms, academics and politicians have contended that youth in ten or even twenty-five years will generate "a coming storm of juvenile violence."[4] In a notable example, Rep. Bill McCollum warned a House of Representatives subcommittee in April 1996 to "brace yourself for the coming generation of 'super-predators,'"imputing criminal tendencies to infants not yet out of their diapers.[5]

Though these pronouncements make good sound bites, they do not match up to the facts. The truth is that the number of juvenile arrests nationwide has declined in recent years. The Federal Bureau of Investigation (FBI) reports that arrests of juveniles for offenses included in the Crime Index decreased by nearly 4 percent from 1993 to 1997, the last year for which final data are available.

---

[4]Council on Crime in America, *The State of Violent Crime in America: A First Report of the Council on Crime in America* (Washington, D.C.: New Citizenship Project, 1996).

[5]House Committee on Economic and Educational Opportunities, Subcommittee on Early Childhood, Youth and Families, *Hearings on the Juvenile Justice and Delinquency Prevention Act,* Serial No. 104-68, 104th Cong., 2d sess., 1996, p. 90 (statement of Rep. Bill McCollum, chairman, Subcommittee on Crime, House Judiciary Committee). Similarly, James Q. Wilson predicted that the first decade of the next century will see "30,000 more young muggers, killers, and thieves than we have now. Get ready." James Q. Wilson, "Crime and Public Policy," in *Crime,* ed. James Q. Wilson and Joan Petersilia (San Francisco: Institute for Contemporary Studies Press, 1995), p. 507. John DiIulio, a Princeton professor who coined the term "superpredator," declared in 1996: "By the year 2010, there will be approximately 270,000 more juvenile super-predators on the streets than there were in 1990." John DiIulio, *How to Stop the Coming Crime Wave* (New York: Manhattan Institute, 1996), p. 1. And James Alan Fox, a Northeastern University academic, forecasted a "blood bath" from juvenile homicide involvement in 2005. James A. Fox, *Trends in Juvenile Violence: A Report to the United States Attorney General on Current and Future Rates of Juvenile Offending* (Boston: Northeastern University Press, 1996).

Juvenile arrests for violent crimes—murder, rape, robbery, and aggravated assault—were down by 6 percent during the same time period.[6] Prof. James Q. Wilson, one of those who predicted a rise in youth crime, conceded in January 1999, "So far, it clearly hasn't happened. . . . That is a good indication of what little all of us know about criminology."[7]

It is true that the drop in reported arrests during the last decade comes after substantial increases in juvenile arrests in some violent offense categories, notably homicide and aggravated assault. While these increases would appear to lend support to those who claim that crime by juveniles is on the rise, relying on arrest data to measure the crime rate is misleading. Arrest data, the only official statistics on youth violence in the United States, overestimate the number of violent acts attributable to youth. As Prof. Franklin Zimring points out, "Younger offenders commit offenses in groups much more often than older offenders, and they are also arrested in groups much more often."[8] Moreover, in the case of arrests for aggravated assault, there are substantial indications that changing police standards, rather than increased violence by adolescents, explain the increased number of arrests in that category.[9]

---

[6]*See* U.S. Department of Justice, Federal Bureau of Investigation, *Uniform Crime Reports for the United States 1997* (Washington, D.C.: U.S. Government Printing Office, 1998), p. 228. *See also* Howard N. Snyder, *Juvenile Arrests 1997* (Washington, D.C.: OJJDP, December 1998), p. 1. Juvenile crime arrest rates declined each year during this five-year period. From 1994 to 1995, juvenile arrests nationwide for violent crimes declined 3 percent. Howard N. Snyder, *Juvenile Arrests 1995* (Washington, D.C.: OJJDP, February 1997), p. 1. From 1995 to 1996, arrests of juveniles under eighteen years of age for violent crimes decreased 5.8 percent. For those under fifteen years of age, arrests for violent crimes decreased 7.2 percent for the same period. U.S. Department of Justice, Federal Bureau of Investigation, *Uniform Crime Reports: Crime in the United States for 1995 and 1996* (Washington, D.C.: U.S. Government Printing Office, 1996), p. 222.

[7]Jacques Steinberg, "Storm Warning: The Coming Crime Wave Is Washed Up," *The New York Times,* January 3, 1999.

[8]Franklin E. Zimring, *American Youth Violence* (New York: Oxford University Press, 1988), p. 18. Further, OJJDP notes that arrest figures overestimate the extent to which juveniles are involved in violent crimes because they are based on the assumption that "each of these arrests involved a different juvenile (i.e., if each juvenile arrested in 1995 for a Violent Crime Index Offense were arrested only once that year—which is very unlikely)." Snyder, *Juvenile Arrests 1995,* p. 4.

[9]Zimring, *American Youth Violence,* pp. 38-45 (analyzing FBI data from 1980 to 1995 to determine trends in arrest rates for aggravated assault). *See generally* U.S. Department of Justice, FBI, *Crime in the United States,* (Washington, D.C.: U.S. Government Printing Office, annual volumes for 1980-1995). Zimring explains:

Even the increases in juvenile homicide arrests do not support measures that target youthful offenders. Eric Lotke and Vincent Shiraldi observe that "the reality is that very few Americans are in personal danger of homicide victimization at the hands of a juvenile. . . [J]ust four cities—Chicago, Los Angeles, New York and Detroit—had a combined total of 929 juvenile homicide arrests in 1994, accounting for 30 percent of the 3,102 juvenile homicide arrests in the nation."[10] Far more serious are killings by adult offenders, who reportedly "commit eleven of twelve homicides, including three-fourths of the murders of children and teen-agers, statistics that are ignored in the furor over 'killer kids.'"[11]

To a large extent, however, the modern-day legend of the coming superpredators exempts itself from the need to face reality. Zimring notes, "To talk of a 'coming storm' creates a riskless environment for getting tough in advance of the future threat. If the crime rate rises, the prediction has been validated. If the crime rate does not rise, the policies that the alarmists put in place can be credited with avoiding the bloodbath. The prediction cannot be falsified, currently or ever."[12]

This environment allows lawmakers and academics to dismiss the current trend, which shows juvenile crime to be on the wane, with dire forebodings. Indeed, Representative McCollum asserted, "Today's drop in crime is only the calm before the coming storm."[13] Such an approach takes a demographic projection—that there will be more teenagers in the future—and wildly extrapolates from studies of chronic delinquency to conclude that a youth crime wave is in the wings. This is phony criminology, relying as it does on a prediction

---

> How assaults are counted and classified is essentially a matter of police discretion. Changing police standards can have a huge impact on statistical trends. For the period since 1980, there is significant circumstantial evidence from many sources that changing police thresholds for when assault should be recorded and when the report should be for aggravated assault are the reason for most of the growth in arrest rates.

Zimring, *American Youth Violence*, p. 39. *See also* Franklin E. Zimring, "American Youth Violence: Issues and Trends," in *Crime and Justice: An Annual Review of Research,* ed. Norval Morris and Michael Tonry (Chicago: University of Chicago Press, 1979).

[10]Eric Lotke and Vincent Shiraldi, *An Analysis of Juvenile Homicides: Where They Occur and the Effectiveness of Adult Court Intervention* (Washington, D.C.: National Center on Institutions and Alternatives and Center on Juvenile and Criminal Justice, 1996), p. 4.

[11]Mike A. Males, "Five Myths, and Why Adults Believe They Are True," *The New York Times,* April 29, 1998, p. G9.

[12]Zimring, *American Youth Violence,* p. 63.

[13]*Hearings on the Juvenile Justice and Delinquency Prevention Act,* p. 89.

technique that is, in Zimring's words, "empty of logical and empirical content." [14] Zimring continues:

> If the argument implied is that the number of homicides or robberies generated by a youth cohort can be easily predicted by its relative size, this is far from obvious in the record of recent American history. The rate of youth violence increased in the late 1980s even as the youth population declined, and the volume of youth violence decreased after 1993 as the youth population grew.[15]

The modern-day legend of the coming superpredators has driven legislative approaches to juvenile and criminal justice, overcoming hard facts and sound research.

A Flawed Response

In response to the perceived increase in violent juvenile crime, between 1992 and 1998 at least forty states, including Maryland, made it easier to try children as adults. Juveniles may be transferred to criminal court in a variety of ways, each of which carries some potential for arbitrary decisionmaking. In particular, African-American and other minority youth may be disproportionately transferred to the criminal courts.

The negative aspects of transferring youth to adult courts are not balanced by concrete results. The proponents of such measures argue that criminal courts can issue harsher sentences, which in turn will deter other youth from committing violent crime. There is no clear indication, however, that children tried as adults receive longer sentences than they would before juvenile court judges or that treating youth as adults actually reduces crime.

---

[14]Zimring, *American Youth Violence,* p. 63.

[15]Ibid. Zimring analyzed census statistics to determine trends in the youth population and then compared youth population trends with the arrest rate trends he identified from FBI data. *See* ibid., pp. 49-65. *See generally* U.S. Department of Commerce, Bureau of the Census, *Current Population Reports: Estimates of the Population of the United States by Age, Sex, and Race* (Washington, D.C.: U.S. Government Printing Office, annual volumes for 1960-1995); U.S. Department of Justice, FBI, *Crime in the United States,* (Washington, D.C.: U.S. Government Printing Office, annual volumes for 1980-1995). Zimring concludes that the "only proper inference to be drawn from knowing that an extra million teenagers will be present at some future time is that there will be a larger group of teenagers. . . . How many muggers or killers will be in that population is not known or predicted . . . ." Zimring, *American Youth Violence,* p. 63.

How Children Are Sent to Adult Courts

The way youth can be moved from the juvenile courts to the criminal courts differs from state to state. In some states, the prosecutor has nearly complete discretion over whether to place a juvenile in the adult system. Other states automatically exclude certain charges from the juvenile court's jurisdiction. In addition, nearly all states give juvenile court judges the discretion to waive their jurisdiction in particularly serious cases.[16]

Such provisions are not new; from their creation, the juvenile courts have always had some mechanism for transferring the most serious offenses to the adult criminal courts.[17] Historically, transfers were subject to judicial discretion and limited to the most serious offenders who in the judgment of the court could not be rehabilitated. The difference is that in recent years, the shift in emphasis from

---

[16] *See* Eric Fritsch and Craig Hemmens, "Juvenile Waiver in the United States, 1979-1995: A Comparison and Analysis of State Waiver Statutes," *Juvenile and Family Court Journal,* Summer 1995, p.23; Lisa A. Cintron, "Rehabilitating the Juvenile Court System: Limiting Juvenile Transfers to Adult Court," *Northwestern University Law Review,* vol. 90 (1996), pp. 1262-71. Another approach to dealing with serious juvenile offenders is a "blended sentencing" system, in which a youthful offender is given some combination of juvenile sanctions and adult punishment. Between 1992 and 1998, sixteen states adopted some form of blended sentencing. *See* Linda J. Collier, "Adult Crime, Adult Time: Outdated Juvenile Laws Thwart Justice," *The Washington Post,* March 9, 1998, p. C5. In Minnesota, for example, compliance with the terms of the juvenile sentence results in the release of the youth without an adult criminal record. *See, for example,* Pam Belluck, "Fighting Youth Crime, Some States Blend Adult and Juvenile Justice," *New York Times,* February 11, 1998, p. A1. For a discussion of different models of blended sentencing statutes, see OJJDP, *State Responses to Serious and Violent Juvenile Crime* (Washington, D.C: National Center for Juvenile Justice, 1996), pp. 11-14.

[17] *See* Barry C. Feld, "The Juvenile Court Meets the Principle of the Offense: Legislative Changes in Juvenile Waiver Statutes," *Journal of Criminal Law and Criminology,* vol. 78 (1987), p. 478. The United States's first juvenile courts were established in the state of Illinois in 1899; by 1945, every U.S. jurisdiction had a juvenile court. *See* Charles W. Thomas and Shay Bilchik, "Prosecuting Juveniles in Criminal Courts: A Legal and Empirical Analysis," *Journal of Criminal Law and Criminology,* vol. 76 (1985), p. 451. For a review of the development of the juvenile justice system in the United States, see generally Sanford J. Fox, "Juvenile Justice Reform: An Historical Perspective," *Stanford Law Review,* vol. 22 (1970), p. 1187.

rehabilitation to punishment and incapacitation has led to a proliferation of transfer provisions.[18]

In Maryland, many children are automatically tried as adults if they are accused of committing a serious crime, such as murder, rape, or armed robbery; depending on the age of the youth, these offenses are automatically excluded from the juvenile court's jurisdiction.[19] A child who is automatically brought before the criminal court under one of these provisions may ask to have his or her case returned to the juvenile court, a procedure often called a "reverse waiver." In deciding a reverse waiver application, the criminal court decides whether a transfer to the juvenile court is "in the interests of the child or society," taking into account the child's age, mental and physical condition, amenability to treatment in a juvenile institution or program, the nature of the offense charged, and the public safety.[20]

Even when Maryland law does not automatically place cases within the jurisdiction of the criminal court, the juvenile court may waive its jurisdiction in any case, even one involving a misdemeanor charge, in which the child is fifteen years of age or older. The juvenile court may also waive jurisdiction over cases involving younger children who are accused of very serious crimes, such as murder or rape.[21] In order to waive jurisdiction under these discretionary provisions, the juvenile court must consider the same five factors the criminal court would consider in a reverse waiver hearing.[22] If, after considering those factors individually and in relation to each other, the court finds that the child "is an unfit subject for juvenile rehabilitative measures," it may waive its jurisdiction and send the juvenile to adult court.[23]

---

[18] *See generally* Barry C. Feld, "The Transformation of the Juvenile Court," *Minnesota Law Review,* vol. 75 (1991), p. 691. Under Illinois law, for example, children charged with controlled substances violations that occur within 1,000 feet of a school or public housing property are automatically transferred into the adult system. *See* 705 Ill. Comp. Stat. 405/5-130(2) (West 1999).

[19] *See* Md. Code Ann., Courts and Judicial Proceedings Article, § 3-804(e).

[20] *See* Md. Ann. Code, Article 27, § 594A. Not all cases are eligible for transfer to the juvenile court. A child is not eligible for a transfer to the juvenile court if he or she has a prior adult criminal conviction or if he or she previously received a transfer to the juvenile court and was adjudicated delinquent. In addition, a sixteen- or seventeen-year-old accused of murder may not be transferred to the juvenile court. *See* ibid. § 594A(b).

[21] *See* Md. Code Ann., Courts and Judicial Proceedings Article, § 3-817.

[22] *See* ibid. § 3-817(d).

[23] Ibid. § 3-817(c), (e).

The Burden on the System

The increased use of transfers create additional burdens on the criminal courts, often without a corresponding increase in resources. The U.S. Department of Justice's Bureau of Justice Statistics reports that the number of delinquency cases judicially waived to criminal court increased 71 percent between 1985 and 1994, from 7,200 to 12,300 cases annually. These figures do not capture the number of children whose cases were automatically sent to the criminal courts.[24]

The Potential for Arbitrary Decisionmaking

Decisions to transfer youth from the juvenile courts to the criminal courts are inherently problematic, underscoring the need to limit such transfers to the truly exceptional cases. Statutory automatic transfer provisions and prosecutorial direct-file provisions can both be abused if prosecutors overcharge a child in order to secure the child's automatic transfer to criminal court. Automatic transfers, in turn, do not allow for an individualized assessment of whether a child can be rehabilitated.[25] Juvenile court judges are best equipped to make such transfer decisions, since they assess each case individually in a setting that allows juveniles and their attorneys to present the background and circumstances of the youth and the alleged offense.[26]

---

[24]*See* Carol J. DeFrances and Kevin J. Strom, *Juveniles Prosecuted in State Criminal Courts* (Washington, D.C.: Bureau of Justice Statistics, March 1997), p. 5.

[25]*See* Mark I. Soler and others, *Representing the Child Client* (Matthew Bender, March 1998), para. 5.03[12][e]; Barry C. Feld, "The Juvenile Court Meets the Principle of the Offense: Legislative Changes in Juvenile Waiver Statutes," *Journal of Criminal Law and Criminology,* vol. 78 (1987), p. 499.

[26]Even the use of judicial waivers is open to challenge, particularly where transfers to criminal court are not limited to the truly exceptional cases. Criminologists have noted that it is not clear that a juvenile court can accurately measure "amenability to treatment" or predict "dangerousness," and some have found that the exercise of discretion may lead to inconsistent, perhaps arbitrary transfer decisions. *See* Jeffrey Fagan and Elizabeth Piper Deschenes, "Determinants of Judicial Waiver Decisions for Violent Juvenile Offenders," *Journal of Criminal Law and Criminology,* vol. 81 (1990), p. 314 (finding inconsistencies in the application of transfer laws); Barry C. Feld, "Reference of Juvenile Offenders for Adult Prosecution: The Legislative Alternative to Asking Unanswerable Questions," *Minnesota Law Review,* vol. 62 (1978), pp. 529-56 (contending that juvenile court judges lack reliable clinical measures of dangerousness or amenability to rehabilitation); Barry C. Feld, "Bad Law Makes Hard Cases: Reflections on Teen-Aged Axe-Murderers, Judicial Activism, and Legislative Default," *Law and Inequality Journal,* vol. 8 (1990), p. 1 (concluding that standardless discretion leads to inconsistent decisions and "justice by geography").

The Disproportionate Impact on Minority Youth

A number of studies have found that minority children are disproportionately waived into criminal court, suggesting that race and ethnicity may influence the decision to try a child as an adult. A December 1995 study by the Maryland Department of Juvenile Justice reported that 73 percent of the cases in which the juvenile court waived jurisdiction involved black youth; according to the U.S. Bureau of the Census, some 27 percent of the state's population is African-American.[27] Studies in Ohio and Minnesota showed similarly disparate results. Of those cases waived to Ohio's adult courts during 1994, 62.6 percent involved black youthful defendants, whereas African-Americans make up just over 11 percent of the state's population. The disparity was even higher in Ohio's six large urban counties, in which between 63.6 percent and 81.8 percent of those transferred to adult court were black.[28] In Minnesota, "minority juveniles comprised nearly nine out of ten (88 percent) of the youths whom prosecutors sought to waive" in 1992, although minorities represent less than 7 percent of Minnesota's population.[29] Similar findings, based on 1990 and 1991 data, have been reported for California, where 34.3 percent of juvenile cases waived involved African-Americans and 60.2 percent were other minorities; Florida, where 60.1 percent of those waived were black juvenile offenders; Missouri, where 70.5 percent of those waived were African-American; Pennsylvania, with black juveniles making up 55.6 percent of juvenile cases waived to adult court; and South Carolina, where African-American juveniles made up 85.7 percent of all waivers.[30]

---

[27] *See* Disproportionate Minority Representation Task Force, *The Disproportionate Representation of African-American Youth at Various Decision Points in the State of Maryland* (Baltimore: Maryland Department of Juvenile Justice, 1995), p. 8; Population Estimates Program, Population Division, U.S. Bureau of the Census, *Estimates of the Population of States by Race and Hispanic Origin: July 1, 1997* (Washington, D.C.: U.S. Bureau of the Census, 1998), p. 1 ("State Population Estimates"), available on <http://www.census.gov>.

[28] *See* Ohio Department of Youth Services, *Juveniles Transferred to Adult Court in Ohio: Calendar Year 1994* (Columbus, Ohio: Ohio Department of Youth Services, 1994), pp. 3-4; State Population Estimates, p. 1.

[29] *See* Marcy Rasmussen Podkopacz and Barry C. Feld, "The End of the Line: An Empirical Study of Judicial Waiver," *Journal of Criminal Law and Criminology,* vol. 86 (1996), p. 470; State Population Estimates, p. 1.

[30] *See* General Accounting Office, *Juvenile Justice: Juveniles Processed in Criminal Court and Case Dispositions* (Washington, D.C.: GAO, 1995), pp. 50-58. Minorities make up just over 20 percent of California's population, with African Americans making up just 7.4 percent of the total. In Florida, 15.4 percent of the population is black; in Missouri, 11.2

The Effect on Sentences and Crime

Lost in the rush to impose harsher sanctions on youthful offenders is whether such measures have any concrete results. "The assumption is that the policy makers believe that criminal courts will be tougher and can serve as a more effective deterrent for juvenile crime," notes the National Council of Juvenile and Family Court Judges. "This assumption is not borne out by the facts."[31]

The first of these assumptions is that the criminal courts are "tougher" on youth, meaning that they will hand down stiffer sentences. Analyzing the sentences received by youth in New York and New Jersey, Jeffrey Fagan observed that efforts to address adolescent crimes in the criminal courts "have been fueled by the expectation of greater accountability (more certain and proportionate punishment) and lengthier sentences in the criminal court" but that "none of these promises has been fulfilled."[32] Fagan concludes that although adolescents transferred to criminal court were more likely to be convicted and to be sentenced to periods of incarceration, offenders whose cases were handled in the juvenile court were punished more swiftly. Furthermore, youth who were sentenced to incarceration received nearly identical sentence lengths regardless of whether they were tried in adult court or juvenile court.[33] Similarly, a study of Texas youths tried in the criminal courts between 1981 and 1993 found that they rarely served sentences that were longer than they could have received in the juvenile courts.[34]

The second assumption is that treating juveniles as adults reduces crime. A study by the National Center for Initiatives and Alternatives compared Connecticut, with the highest juvenile-to-adult transfer rate in the United States, with Colorado, the state with the lowest rate of transfers of juveniles to adult courts. The youth crime rate was the same in each state. Similarly, studies of violent juvenile crime rates in Idaho, Florida, and New York found that the adoption of waiver or transfer

---

percent; in Pennsylvania, 9.7 percent; and in South Carolina, African Americans represent 30 percent of the population. *See* State Population Estimates, p. 1.

[31]National Council of Juvenile and Family Court Judges, *Where We Stand: An Action Plan for Dealing with Violent Juvenile Crime* (Reno, Nevada: National Council of Juvenile and Family Court Judges, n.d.), p. 2.

[32]Jeffrey Fagan, "The Comparative Advantage of Juvenile Versus Criminal Court Sanctions on Recidivism Among Adolescent Felony Offenders," *Law and Policy,* vol. 18 (1996), p. 98.

[33]Ibid., p. 100.

[34]*See* Eric J. Fritsch, Tory J. Caeti, and Craig Hemmens, "Spare the Needle But Not the Punishment: The Incarceration of Waived Youth in Texas Prisons," *Crime and Delinquency,* vol. 42 (1996), p. 593.

statutes in each state did not have a deterrent effect on violent crimes.[35] Fagan's study of New York and New Jersey youth concluded that "criminal court punishment was not a more effective strategy for crime control."[36] In the words of Dr. Barry Krisberg, president of the National Council on Crime and Delinquency, "There is no evidence that either enhanced prosecution or stiffer penalties are preventing violent and serious youth crime."[37]

The findings of Fagan and others suggest, in fact, that juveniles prosecuted as adults are more likely to commit crimes in the future than their peers in the juvenile system are, leading the Association of the Bar of the City of New York's Committee on Juvenile Justice to conclude:

> Prosecuting more youths in the adult system, and increasing the time they will spend in adult facilities, is resoundingly unwise. Extensive research demonstrates that teenagers who are prosecuted in the adult system are more often re-arrested and are re-arrested for more serious offenses than those teenagers who are prosecuted as juveniles. Treating juveniles as adults will not serve to reduce crime or increase community safety but may actually have the opposite effect.[38]

---

[35]*See* Richard Lacayo, "Teen Crime," *Time,* July 21, 1997, p. 28; Eric L. Jensen and Linda Metsger, "Waiver of Juveniles to Criminal Court," *Idaho Law Review,* vol. 31 (1994), p. 174; Donna M. Bishop and others, "The Transfer of Juveniles to Criminal Court: Does It Make a Difference?," *Crime and Delinquency,* vol. 42 (1996), p.183; Simon I. Singer and David McDowell, "Criminalizing Delinquency: The Deterrent Effects of the New York Juvenile Offender Law," *Law and Society Review*, vol. 22 (1988), p. 521. The authors of the Florida study concluded:

> Overall, the results suggest that transfer in Florida has had little deterrent value. Nor has it produced any incapacitative benefits that enhance public safety. Although incarcerated youth were more likely to be incarcerated and to be incarcerated for longer periods than those retained in the juvenile justice system, they quickly reoffended at a higher rate than the nontransferred controls, thereby negating any incapacitative benefits that might have been achieved in the short run.

Bishop and others, "Does It Make a Difference?," p. 183.

[36]Fagan, "Court Sanctions," p. 100.

[37]Mark Dowie, "When Kids Commit Adult Crimes, Some Say They Should Do Adult Time, *California Lawyer,* vol. 13 (1993), p. 57.

[38]Committee on Juvenile Justice, "Report on Governor Pataki's Juvenile Justice Reform Proposals," *The Record of the Association of the Bar of the City of New York,* vol. 52 (May 1997), p. 451.

In short, the transfer of youth to adult courts falls short of meeting either promise. Prosecuting adolescents as adults does not ensure lengthier prison sentences for those who receive time, nor does it measurably reduce crime.

The Consequences of Being Tried as an Adult

Once transferred to adult court, the most immediate consequence for many children—even those ultimately acquitted of the charges against them—is detention in adult jails while they await trial. Whether or not they are ultimately found innocent, many of these children face the prospect of spending six months to a year or more, a significant portion of their formative adolescent years, behind bars. "Being charged as an adult, it can take half your life away," said Eddie L., a seventeen-year-old in the Prince George's County Correctional Center.[39] (In this report, the names of all youth have been changed to protect their privacy.)

In Baltimore, prosecutors are not involved in the initial charging of defendants, contrary to the practice in the majority of U.S. states. Instead, the task of preparing the charges falls to the police, whose decision may go unreviewed for up to one month. According to a report released in December 1998 by the Criminal Courts Technical Assistance Project, Baltimore police often charge defendants with crimes more serious than the evidence supports—charges that are often dropped when the defendants go to trial.[40]

These practices come at a time when Baltimore's courts are increasingly backlogged. A *Baltimore Sun* investigation found in February 1998 that 150 adult inmates at the Baltimore City Detention Center had been held for more than one year without a trial; an official count taken at the end of June 1997 found that 700 inmates were in the detention center for six months or more without a trial.[41] That same month, state prosecutors dropped charges against a rape suspect because they had lost contact with the victim in the nearly two years since the suspect's arrest, and a circuit court judge dismissed charges against another inmate who had been

---

[39]Human Rights Watch interview, P.G. County Correctional Center, July 23, 1998.

[40]The *Baltimore Sun* reported in December 1998 that prosecutors declined to try 60 percent of the misdemeanors charged by city police in 1997. In May 1998, 23 percent of the criminal cases on the docket of the circuit court were never prosecuted, either for lack of evidence or because charges were dropped as part of plea bargains. The circuit court tries felony cases and misdemeanor jury trials. *See* Caitlin Francke, "Proposal Aims to Unclog Courts; City Prosecutors, Not Police Would Decide on Charges," *The Baltimore Sun,* December 10, 1998, p. 1A.

[41]*See* Ivan Penn, "150 City Suspects Jailed over a Year Waiting Trial; Rape Defendant Freed in Part Because Case Is Nearly 2 Years Old," *The Baltimore Sun,* February 3, 1998, p. 1A.

held for more than sixteen months with no trial.[42] Juveniles held in Maryland's jails face the prospect of six months to a year or more in detention before their cases come to trial.

OJJDP notes that such delays "should be viewed from the perspective of an adolescent offender. Professional standards suggest that even the longest case should be processed within 90 days. Yet, a 90-day process means that a 14-year-old offender will wait the equivalent of a summer vacation for services or sanctions."[43] Juvenile law experts and developmental psychologists concur that children's cases must be resolved rapidly if any sanctions imposed are to serve a meaningful rehabilitative purpose.[44]

If found guilty, children tried as adults may be subjected to mandatory minimum sentences, "three-strikes" laws, and "truth-in-sentencing" laws, provisions which are intended to increase the prison terms imposed on convicted offenders and reduce their eligibility for parole.[45] In fourteen states, juvenile

---

[42]*See* Ivan Penn, "Suspect in Jail Nearly 2 Years Sees His Rape Charges Dropped; State Cited Length of Case, Victim's Disappearance," *The Baltimore Sun,* February 3, 1998, p. 6A; Brenda J. Buote, "Charges Against Prisoner Dismissed; Detention Center Inmate Had Been Held 16 Months," *The Baltimore Sun,* February 19, 1998, p. 3B. A third inmate was reportedly held for almost twenty months before he accepted a guilty plea. *See* Ivan Penn, "Inmate Jailed Without Trial for 20 Months Pleads Guilty; He Admits to Burglary in Plea Agreement," *The Baltimore Sun,* February 6, 1998, p. 2B.

[43]U.S. Department of Justice, Office of Justice Programs, Office of Juvenile Justice and Delinquency Prevention, *Delays in Juvenile Court Processing of Delinquency Cases* (Washington, D.C.: OJJDP, 1997), p. 1.

[44]Delays in bringing cases to trial do not only hamper efforts at rehabilitation. Where criminal proceedings are so protracted that charges must be dropped or dismissed, these delays hurt the victims of crimes by denying them redress.

[45]*See, for example,* Michael Tony, *Sentencing Matters* (Oxford University Press: New York, 1995) (mandatory minimum sentences); Human Rights Watch, "Cruel and Unusual: Disproportionate Sentences for New York Drug Offenders," *A Human Rights Watch Short Report,* vol. 9, no. 2, March 1997 (analyzing the impact of mandatory minimum sentences for drug offenders in New York State); California Department of Corrections, "Count of Prisoners Sentenced for Third and Second Strike Cases," June 30, 1998 ("three strikes" laws); Kevin R. Reitz, "Federal Influence in State Cases: Sentencing, Prosecution, and Procedure—The Federal Role in Sentencing Law and Policy," *Annals of the American Academy of Political and Social Science,* January 1996, p. 117 (describing the "truth-in-sentencing" provision of the federal Violent Crime Control and Law Enforcement Act of 1994, which requires states to adopt measures to ensure that violent offenders "shall not serve less than 85 percent of the sentence imposed").

offenders charged as adults are among those who are barred for life from voting.[46] In many cases, they will emerge without a high school diploma. All "will carry forever the stamp of a convicted felon, making it difficult to find employment."[47]

International Standards

International standards recognize that children, a particularly vulnerable group, are entitled to special care and protection because they are still developing physically, mentally, and emotionally.[48] With this in mind, international human rights documents strongly encourage states to develop specialized laws, procedures, authorities, and institutions for handling the cases of children in conflict with the law.[49]

Whether or not they have established juvenile courts, states parties to human rights treaties are obligated to afford children the basic guarantees of a fair trial, including the right to be presumed innocent until proven guilty, to be informed promptly and directly of the charges against them, to have legal or other appropriate assistance in the preparation of their defense, to have the matter determined without delay by a competent, independent, and impartial authority, not to be compelled to give testimony or to confess guilt, to have adverse witnesses examined, and to obtain the participation and examination of witnesses on their

---

[46]Maryland permanently disenfranchises those convicted of a second felony. *See* Human Rights Watch and The Sentencing Project, *Losing the Vote: The Impact of Felony Disenfranchisement Laws in the United States* (New York: Human Rights Watch & The Sentencing Project, October 1998), pp. 4-5.

[47]Alex Kotlowitz, "Their Crimes Don't Make Them Adults," *The New York Times Magazine,* February 13, 1994, p. 41.

[48]*See, for example,* Universal Declaration of Human Rights, Article 25(2), G.A. Res. 217A(III), U.N. Doc. A/810, p. 71 (1948). Similarly, the United States Supreme Court has recognized that

> Adolescents, particularly in the early middle and teen years, are more vulnerable, more impulsive, and less self-disciplined than adults. Crimes committed by youths may be just as harmful to victims as those committed by older persons, but they deserve less punishment because adolescents may have less capacity to control their conduct and to think in long-range terms than adults.

Eddings v. Oklahoma, 455 U.S. 104, 115 n.11 (1982).

[49]Article 40(3) of the Convention on the Rights of the Child calls upon states "to promote the establishment of laws, procedures, authorities, and institutions specifically applicable to children alleged as, accused of, or recognized as having infringed the penal law." *See also* U.N. Standard Minimum Rules for the Administration of Juvenile Justice, Article 1.4, G.A. Res. 40/33, 40 U.N. GAOR Supp. (No. 53), p. 207, U.N. Doc. A/40/53 (1985).

own behalf. If found to have infringed the penal law, children must be afforded the right to have the adverse decision reviewed by a higher tribunal.[50]

In addition to these basic due process guarantees, children in the justice system benefit from additional protections mandated by international standards. In particular, states are required to offer a range of alternatives to institutionalization. The imprisonment of a child should always be a measure of last resort and for the shortest appropriate period of time.[51]

Human Rights Watch believes that, interpreting these standards in practical terms, there should be a strong presumption in favor of adjudicating children's cases in the juvenile justice system. A decision to transfer a case from the juvenile justice system to the ordinary criminal courts should be limited to extraordinarily severe cases. Such a decision should be made by a judge rather than a prosecutor. The judge should consider the nature and the seriousness of the alleged offense, the age and history of the child, and his or her amenability to treatment. Transfers to the criminal courts should not be mandatory under law and should not be made in an arbitrary or in a discriminatory manner. In accordance with international standards, the decision of the judge should be subject to review by a higher tribunal; the procedures for the review of transfer decisions by a higher tribunal should protect the child's right to a fair trial without undue delay in adjudication and without deprivation of liberty beyond the shortest appropriate period of time.

---

[50]*See* International Covenant on Civil and Political Rights, Article 14(5), *opened for signature* December 19, 1966, 999 U.N.T.S. 171 (entered into force March 23, 1976); Convention on the Rights of the Child, Article 40(b).

[51]*See* Convention on the Rights of the Child, Articles 40(4) and 37(b). *See also* U.N. Standard Minimum Rules for the Administration of Juvenile Justice, Articles 17-19.

III. THE DETENTION OF CHILDREN IN ADULT JAILS

Being here with adults, that ain't going to rehabilitate me, it just teaching me to be a better criminal. They looking to lock me up, throw away the key, leave me with no hope. I need to break out the cycle, get me some services and treatment so I can be a productive member of society. Being an adult, that's right around the corner. I be asking for treatment, but I'm seventeen, six foot three, 200 pounds. I still got the mind of a minor, but they look to the body first.

—James S. (not his actual name), interviewed in the Montgomery County Detention Center, July 30, 1999

Those children who are not released on bail or placed in juvenile institutions are held in county jails while they await trial.[52] While they may ask to be transferred to juvenile facilities, such requests are rarely granted. As a result, in Baltimore, where we documented the most severe conditions of confinement, over 150 juveniles charged as adults are held in the city detention center, an aging facility that has been operating above its original rated capacity for at least ten years.[53] At midyear 1995, according to figures from the U.S. Department of Justice Bureau of Justice Statistics, Maryland had 200 inmates under the age of eighteen in its state and federal correctional facilities, an increase of almost 30 percent in five years.[54]

---

[52]Maryland law provides that "a child may not be detained at, or committed or transferred to a penal instititution or other facility used primarily for the confinement of adults charged with or convicted of a crime" unless the child is being proceeded against as an adult. If that is the case, "the child shall promptly be transferred to the appropriate officer or adult detention facility in accordance with the law governing the detention of persons charged with a crime." Md. Code Ann., Courts and Judicial Proceedings Article, § 3-816(b). *See also* ibid. § 3-823(a).

[53]The U.S. Department of Justice'sBureau of Justice Statistics records that the Baltimore City's detention center operated at 110 percent of capacity in 1988, 118 percent in 1993, and 129 percent in 1994. U.S. Department of Justice, Office of Justice Programs, Bureau of Justice Statistics, *Correctional Populations in the United States, 1995* (Washington, D.C.: Bureao of Justice Statistics, 1997), p. 25.

[54]Ibid., p. 68. For comparison, OJJDP reports that 715 juveniles were held in public juvenile facilities as of February 15, 1995. U.S. Department of Justice, Office of Justice Programs, Office of Juvenile Justice and Delinquency Prevention, *States at a Glance: Juveniles in Public Facilities, 1995* (Washington, D.C.: OJJDP, November 1997), p. 2.

This increase parallels a national trend. Across the United States, the Office of Juvenile Justice and Delinquency Prevention has documented a 14 percent increase between 1985 and 1995 in the number of children held in adult jails.[55] Nationwide, the Bureau of Justice Statistics estimates that an average of some 6,000 children were held as adults in jails each day in 1995.[56]

In Maryland, individuals who are charged with a crime and who cannot afford (or are not granted) bail are held in pretrial detention in one of twenty-three county jails or in the Baltimore City Detention Center. In fiscal year 1997, some 7,160 persons were held in Maryland's local detention centers awaiting trial or sentencing;[57] between 200 and 300 of that total were juveniles.

With the exception of Baltimore City's jail, Maryland's jails are maintained by the county governments and are usually placed under the supervision of the local sheriffs' offices. Largely in response to an inmate class action lawsuit, the Baltimore City Detention Center has been maintained by the state since 1991; it falls under the purview of the state Department of Public Safety and Correctional Services, the state agency primarily responsible for Maryland's prisons.

Many of Maryland's jails do not separate children from adult inmates. In Frederick and Washington Counties, for example, jail staff told us that children are routinely commingled with adults. Even in the largest facilities, we found that children are exposed to adult inmates to a degree that would not meet the "sight and sound" separation standard that would be required if these children were charged in the juvenile courts. Juveniles may be housed with adults even in the largest facilities.

Children and jail administrators alike frequently expressed the view that juveniles should not be held in jails together with adults. "You need to get the juveniles out of here," Terence B., age seventeen, told us during an interview at the Baltimore City Detention Center, where he had been detained for more than six months. "We can't handle what the adults can handle. We ain't ready for that."[58] Similarly, Commissioner LaMont Flanagan told us during an interview at the

---

[55]*Delinquency Cases Waived to Criminal Court,* p. 1; *OJJDP Annual Report* (Washington, D.C.: OJJDP, 1998), p. 44.

[56]*Correctional Populations in the United States, 1995,* p. 26.

[57]For a breakdown of average daily population by jail for fiscal years 1994 through 1997, see Maryland General Assembly, *Maryland's Criminal and Juvenile Justice Process* (Annapolis, Maryland: Maryland Department of Legislative Services, 1998), pp. 47-48.

[58]Human Rights Watch interview, Baltimore City Detention Center, April 30, 1999.

Baltimore City Detention Center, "I think these kids should be in juvenile facilities, but the statutes and laws are going in a different direction."[59]

The Strain on the System

The impact of housing children in adult jails goes beyond the increase in sheer numbers. Children often have more incentive than adults to go to trial, meaning that jails are faced with the prospect of housing younger detainees for longer periods of time. In Baltimore, the detention center staff estimate that juvenile inmates spend an average of six months in detention before their cases are resolved. Elsewhere in the country, studies have found that juveniles charged as adults spend more time in pretrial detention than do their counterparts who face charges in the juvenile courts.[60]

Juvenile justice experts note that the detention of adolescents "raises complex issues of housing, special program needs, individualized attention, impulsivity, erratic behavior, and unpredictable situational reactions."[61] In fact, "[m]isconduct by young inmates is, to some extent, linked to their development as adolescents. Staff reponses based on adult patterns of misconduct are likely to be less effective in managing juveniles."[62] Without the specialized training necessary to deal with adolescents, many jail guards are simply unprepared to handle juveniles. An official with the South Carolina Department of Corrections has noted that, in adult facilities, "[a]ll of our policies and procedures are developed with the understanding that adults understand the consequences. Juvenile offenders don't

---

[59]Human Rights Watch interview with LaMont Flanagan, commissioner, Division of Pretrial Detention and Services, Maryland Department of Public Safety and Correctional Services, Baltimore, Maryland, May 11, 1999.

[60]For example, a recent study found that sentencing for juveniles in criminal court took an average of 145 days from the date of arrest; in comparison, youths charged with comparable offenses in juvenile court waited 100 days to be sentenced. *See* Jeffrey Fagan, "Separating the Men from the Boys: The Comprative Advantage of Juvenile Versus Criminal Court Sanctions on Recidivism Among Adolescent Offenders," in James C. Howell and others, eds., *A Sourcebook: Serious, Violent, Chronic Juvenile Offenders* (1995), p. 245.

[61]Fred Cohen, professor emeritus, School of Criminal Justice, State University of New York, quoted in "Legal Expert Urges Proactive Approach to Juveniles Serving as Adults," *The Corrections Professional,* December 11, 1998, p. 3.

[62]Dale Parent and others, *Key Legislative Issues in Criminal Justice: Transferring Serious Juvenile Offenders to Adult Courts* (Washington: National Institute of Justice, 1997), p. 5.

understand that. Four weeks is an eternity for them. They don't understand time."[63]

International standards recognize that a child's case should be resolved expeditiously and without unnecessary delay, a concern which is even more pronounced when the child is detained. Children held in adult detention facilities are deprived of the benefit of specialized programming that would be available to them if they were held in juvenile institutions.

For these reasons, the American Jail Association recognized in 1993: "The care and legal requirements of housing juveniles . . . require specially trained staff and specially designed programming not readily available in an adult facility."[64] Barry Stanton, the Prince George's County Correctional Center's director, puts it more simply. "We're not trained to be babysitters," he states. "Don't ask me to be a mental health expert, a teacher, a disciplinarian for juveniles. It's not my job."[65]

The Risks to Children's Safety and Well-Being

Because of the nature of a jail, detained children may be at risk of harm from other juveniles. Mark Soler, president of the Youth Law Center, contends that "it makes an enormous difference" whether youths are held in a jail or a juvenile detention facility:

> Proper juvenile detention facilities are quite different from adult jails. Juvenile detention facilities have the space to classify children who are admitted, and therefore to separate potentially predatory youth from children who are particularly vulnerable. Jails can't do that—they generally have one cell or one cellblock for the juveniles, so dangerous youth and vulnerable children are thrown in together, often with disastrous consequences.[66]

---

[63]Bill Sturgeon, special assistant to the director, South Carolina Department of Corrections, quoted in "The Great Debate: Should Juveniles Be Housed in Adult Institutions?," *The Corrections Professional,* February 6, 1998, pp. 1-6.

[64]American Jail Association, Resolution on Juveniles in Jails, May 1993.

[65]Human Rights Watch interview with Barry L. Stanton, director, Prince George's County Correctional Center, Upper Marlboro, Maryland, July 23, 1998.

[66]Mark I. Soler, Testimony Before the Senate Youth Violence Subcommittee, Senate Judiciary Committee, on the Core Requirements of the Juvenile Justice Act and the "Violent Juvenile and Repeat Offender Act of 1997," May 6, 1997, p. 2.

Children detained in jails are also at risk of harm from the adult inmate population. Commenting on a proposed federal initiative that would allow juvenile offenders to be housed with adults, Shay Bilchik, administrator of the Office of Juvenile Justice and Delinquency Prevention at the U.S. Department of Justice, stated: "We believe that the standard proposed by [Senators Hatch and Sessions] would inevitably lead to increased physical assaults on juveniles, including sexual abuse and other attendant harm, new lawsuits and a further blurring of the differences between the criminal and juvenile justice systems."[67]

These factors may lead to serious emotional consequences for children held in adult facilities. The most vulnerable children often "have little choice but to enter protective custody, which is usually a separate, secure housing unit in which they spend a great deal of time in isolation—a setting that is especially conducive to suicidal behavior."[68] In fact, children held in jails are up to eight times more likely to commit suicide than those held in juvenile detention centers.[69] Testifying before the Senate Judiciary Committee's Subcommittee on Youth Violence, Soler stated:

> Children who get arrested often feel like their world is ending—they are humiliated, their parents are angry, their friends will all find out. If they have been using alcohol or drugs, these feelings are exacerbated. If they are put in a room at the end of a hallway, as they often are with the sheriff's intention of keeping them away from adult inmates, then depression and isolation feed on each other, they feel life is no longer worth living, and they seek to end it.[70]

As Stanton points out, "We need to understand the impact, the real costs attached to locking up juveniles in adult detention centers. It increases overcrowding in already overcrowded facilities. These juveniles should really be going to a juvenile facility and, if necessary, transferred to an adult facility when they turn eighteen. We have to remember, these are young offenders."[71]

---

[67]Charles Levendosky, "A Road Back to the Dark Ages of Prison Policy," *The Sun,* Feb. 10, 1998, p. 17A.

[68]Dale Parent and others, *Key Legislative Issues,* p. 5.

[69]*See* Office of Juvenile Justice and Delinquency Prevention, *Juveniles in Adult Jails and Lockups: It's Your Move* (Washington, D.C.: OJJDP, 1985), p. 3.

[70]Soler, Testimony before the Senate Youth Violence Subcommittee, p.2.

[71]Human Rights Watch interview with Barry Stanton, July 23, 1998.

Legal Standards

United States Law and Policy

In the case of *convicted adult* prisoners, conditions of confinement violate the United States Constitution if they constitute "cruel and unusual punishment" under the Eighth Amendment.[72] In assessing whether a particular condition or practice is cruel and unusual, the federal courts examine whether the condition results in an "unecessary and wanton infliction of pain" and whether the officials acted with deliberate indifference to the rights of the inmate.[73] Pretrial detainees benefit from greater protections because they have not been convicted of a crime. Innocent until proven guilty, they may not be confined under conditions that "amount to punishment." Such confinement violates the due process clause of the Fourteenth Amendment and the due process protections contained in the Maryland Declaration of Rights.[74]

The U.S. Department of Justice has the statutory authority to begin either a a civil lawsuit or a criminal prosecution to address civil rights violations by state officials. Acting under the Civil Rights of Institutionalized Persons Act (CRIPA), the department may investigate allegations of constitutional rights violations in a state's jails and prisons. The department may also bring suit under a provision of the Violent Crime Control and Law Enforcement Act of 1994 that outlaws a "pattern or practice" of civil rights abuses by law enforcement officers. Finally, the

[72]*Rhodes v. Chapman,* 452 U.S. 347 (1981). The Eighth Amendment to the U.S. Constitution provides: "Excessive bail shall not be required, nor excessive fines imposed, nor cruel and unusual punishments inflicted."

[73]*Wilson v. Seiter,* 111 S. Ct. 2321 (1991).

[74]*Bell v. Wolfish,* 441 U.S. 520 (1979). The Fourteenth Amendment's due process clause provides: "nor shall any State deprive any person of life, liberty, or property, without due process of law." Under the Maryland due process clause, "no man ought to be taken or imprisoned or desseized of his freehold, liberties or privileges, or outlawed, or exiled, or, in any manner, destroyed, or deprived of his life, liberty or property, but by the judgment of his peers, or by the Law of the land." Maryland Constitution, Article 24 (1981). Although state law may provide greater protections than the minimum established by the U.S. Constitution, *see generally* William J. Brennan, "State Constitutions and the Protections of Individual Rights," *Harvard Law Review,* vol. 90 (1977), p. 489; James G. Exum, "Rediscovering State Constitutions," *North Carolina Law Review,* vol. 70 (1992), p. 1741 Maryland's courts have largely interpreted the protections of the Maryland Declaration of Rights to be virtually identical to their federal counterparts in the Bill of Rights, *see* Stephen J. Shapiro, "Suits Against State Officials for Damages for Violations of Constitutional Rights: Comparing Maryland and Federal Law," 23 U. Balt. L. Rev. 423, 424-25 (1994).

department may criminally prosecute a person who violates an inmate's constitutional rights while acting "under color of state law."

Civil Enforcement Under the Civil Rights of Institutionalized Persons Act

The Civil Rights of Institutionalized Persons Act (CRIPA), enacted in 1980, authorizes the U.S. attorney general to investigate and begin litigation whenever she has reasonable cause to believe that state detainees are being subjected to egregious or flagrant violations of their constitutional rights.[75] This statute also gives the attorney general the right to intervene in ongoing civil rights litigation in the federal courts.[76]

Between 1980 and late April 1999, the Department of Justice opened formal investigations or had taken court action in cases involving 106 jails, thirty-seven prisons, and ninety-nine juvenile facilities. It secured consent decrees or settlement agreements with thirty-four jails, thirteen prisons, and sixty-eight juvenile facilities.[77] In 1996, the department opened a formal investigation into Louisiana's four secure juvenile institutions, following the release of Human Rights Watch's 1995 report *Confinement of Children in Louisiana.* As a result of this investigation, the department intervened in litigation that remains pending before the federal court. The department opened a similar investigation into eleven institutions in Georgia following Human Rights Watch's publication of *Modern Capital of Human Rights?: Abuses in the State of Georgia* in 1996, negotiating a settlement agreement with the State of Georgia in early 1998.[78]

---

[75]Civil Rights of Institutionalized Persons Act, 42 U.S.C. § 1997a(a).

[76]Ibid. § 1997c.

[77]Of the cases listed, the DOJ has closed investigations in fifty jails, twenty-eight prisons, and twenty juvenile facilities. In several cases, the number of facilities initially investigated under CRIPA was lower than the number of facilities covered by the resulting consent decree. For example, the DOJ initially investigated eight juvenile facilities in Puerto Rico; twenty are covered by the CRIPA consent decree. Similarly, the DOJ initially investigated eight juvenile facilities in Kentucky and nine in Georgia; it eventually secured consent decrees covering thirteen Kentucky facilities and thirty-one in Georgia. Letter from Dana Schoenberg, staff attorney, Special Litigation Section, Civil Rights Division, U.S. Department of Justice, May 3, 1999.

[78]*See* Letter from Isabelle Katz Pinzler, acting assistant attorney general, Civil Rights Division, U.S. Department of Justice, to Mike Foster, governor, State of Louisiana, June 18, 1997; Letter from Bill Lann Lee, acting assistant attorney general, Civil Rights Division, U.S. Department of Justice, to Zell Miller, governor, State of Georgia, February 13, 1998; Memorandum of Agreement Between the United States and the State of Georgia Concerning Georgia Juvenile Justice Facilities, March 31, 1998.

"Pattern or Practice" Lawsuits

In addition to its authority under CRIPA, the department may act to protect the constitutional rights of detainees under another civil rights statute, added by the Violent Crime Control and Law Enforcement Act of 1994. Codified at Section 14141 of Title 42 of the United States Code, the statute provides that it is unlawful for any governmental authority or person acting on behalf of any governmental authority "to engage in any pattern or practice of conduct by law enforcement officers . . . that deprives persons of rights, privileges, or immunities secured or protected by the Constitution or laws of the United States."[79]

The provision appears to require a lower burden of proof than that required under CRIPA, which requires a pattern or practice of "egregious or flagrant conditions" causing grievous harm. Under Section 14141, the pattern or practice need not necessarily be "egregious" or "flagrant"; it is sufficient to show that the pattern or practice deprived a person of his or her constitutional rights or other rights secured by federal law. In addition, the department may bring suit under Section 14141 without the extensive prior consultation with the relevant department of corrections that CRIPA requires.

As used in Section 14141, "law enforcement officers" includes the corrections officers in Maryland's jails, all of whom are employees of either the local sheriffs' departments or (in the case of the Baltimore City Detention Center) the Maryland Department of Public Safety and Correctional Services. Accordingly, if it were to investigate conditions of detention in Maryland's jails, the U.S. Department of Justice could employ Section 14141 to supplement its authority under CRIPA.[80]

Criminal Prosecution

Finally, the department may initiate a criminal prosecution based upon two general civil rights provisions, sections 241 and 242 of Title 18 of the United States Code. Nevertheless, the high evidentiary burden required by these laws makes it extremely difficult to convict someone for violating a detainee's constitutional rights. To secure conviction of a public official, the department must prove that the

---

[79]42 U.S.C. § 14141(a).

[80]The department has employed Section 14141 in a number of corrections settings, including its Georgia and Louisiana investigations. In addition, it noted in an investigation of Michigan's prisons that "the pattern or practice of sexual abuse of women inmates by guards" violates both Section 14141 and CRIPA. Letter from Deval Patrick, assistant attorney general, Civil Rights Division, U.S. Department of Justice, to John Engler, governor, State of Michigan, March 27, 1995.

official had the "specific intent" to deprive an inmate of a constitutional right.[81] The specific intent requirement poses a substantial burden for the department because it must show that an official knowingly and willfully participated in violating a prisoner's constitutional right.[82]

Private Lawsuits and the Prison Litigation Reform Act

Individual inmates may bring their own lawsuits to challenge their conditions of confinement.[83] Until recently, in fact, many abusive practices were corrected as the result of consent decrees or other settlements reached after inmates (often represented by nonprofit legal organizations or *pro bono* attorneys) brought class action lawsuits on behalf of themselves and all other similarly situated persons. In April 1996, however, President Clinton signed the Prison Litigation Reform Act (PRLA) into law, dramatically limiting the ability of individuals, nongovernmental organizations, and the Department of Justice to challenge abusive prison conditions through litigation.[84] The act invalidates any settlement that does not include an explicit finding or statement that the conditions challenged in the lawsuit violate a federal statute or the U.S. Constitution. Because prison authorities never willingly admit such violations, such findings are extremely rare. This requirement is likely to make it difficult for parties to reach a settlement in future prison or jail reform suits, particularly because explicit findings of violations would make correctional officials vulnerable to private civil suits. In the words of Mark Soler, the result is that the act "make[s] it difficult, if not impossible, for prisoners to bring federal civil rights lawsuits to protect themselves from unconstitutional conditions of confinement."[85]

---

[81]*See Screws v. United States,* 325 U.S. 91, 103 (1945); *United States v. Guest,* 383 U.S. 745, 760 (1966).

[82]*See Screws,* 325 U.S. at 101-103.

[83]Such suits are often brought under the Civil Rights Act of 1871, as amended, which authorizes legal action against "[e]very person who, under color of any statute, ordinance, regulation, custom or usage . . . subjects, or causes to be subjected, any citizen of the United States or any other person within the jurisdiction thereof to the deprivation of any rights, privileges, or immunities secured by the Constitution and laws." 42 U.S.C. § 1983 (as amended by Pub. L. No. 104-317, § 309(c), 110 Stat. 3853 (1996)).

[84]The Prisoner Litigation Reform Act was enacted as Title VIII of the Omnibus Consolidated Recissions and Appropriations Act of 1996, Pub. L. No. 104-134, 110 Stat. 1321 (April 26, 1996), and is codified at 18 U.S.C. § 3226.

[85]Mark Soler, president, Youth Law Center, quoted in *Proceedings from the National Conference on Juvenile Detention*, December 1996, p. 31.

Between January and March 1997, four of the five state-run correctional facilities in Maryland successfully applied to have consent decrees dissolved.[86] In Baltimore, the Department of Public Safety and Correctional Services has filed a motion to vacate the consent decree that has regulated the Baltimore City Detention Center since 1976.

Class Action Litigation at the Baltimore City Detention Center

Detainees of the Baltimore City Detention Center filed a class action suit, known as *Collins v. Schoonfield,* in the federal district court in 1971 to challenge the conditions of their confinement.[87] In 1976, they initiated a second class action suit, filed under the name *Duvall v. Schaefer,* to challenge overcrowding.[88] The district court approved the first of a series of consent decrees in these cases in 1977.

In 1981, the detainees and the city agreed to revise and consolidate the *Collins* and *Duvall* consent decrees.[89] The State of Maryland took over the administration of the jail in July 1991.[90] In 1993, the inmates and the state agreed once again to revise the decree.[91] The 1993 Revised Consolidated Decree remained in effect until October 31, 1997, when the district court ordered enforcement of the decree suspended.[92]

---

[86]Kate Shatzkin, "4 Md. Prisons Freed from Consent Decrees; A 1995 Act of Congress Led to Termination After More than a Decade," *The Baltimore Sun,* Mar. 18, 1997, p. 1B.

[87]*Collins v. Schoonfield,* 344 F. Supp. 257 (D. Md. 1972) (finding that conditions in the city jail violated inmates' constitutionally protected rights).

[88]*Duvall v. Schaefer,* Civil Action No. K-76-1255 (D. Md. docketed Aug. 24, 1976) (initiated by a June 14, 1976, letter from inmate Jerome Duvall to the federal district court). *See also Duvall v. Schaefer,* Civil Action No. K-76-1255, 1988 U.S. Dist. LEXIS 18298 (D. Md. Aug. 30, 1998) (1988 Revised Consolidated Decree).

[89]Since that time, the combined case has been known as "*Duvall v.*" the sitting governor (currently Parris D. Glendening).

[90]House Bill No. 1059, 1991 Laws of Maryland ch. 59.

[91]*Duvall v. Schaefer,* Civil Action No. K-76-1255 (D. Md. July 9, 1993) (1993 Revised Consolidated Decree).

[92]*See generally* Frank M. Dunbaugh, "Prospecting for Prospective Relief: The Story of Seeking Compliance with a Federal Court Decree Mandating Humane Conditions of Confinement in the Baltimore City Jail," *The Prison Journal,* Fall-Winter 1990, pp. 57-73; Plaintiff's Memorandum in Opposition to the Defendant's Motion to Terminate the 1993 Revised Consolidated Decree, *Duvall v. Glendening,* No. JFM-94-2541, pp. 3-15 (D. Md. filed July 30, 1998) (summarizing the history of the litigation).

The 1993 decree governs the detention of all detainees, including those under the age of eighteen.[93] With regard to juveniles, the decree requires that juveniles be housed separately from adults and mandates that the detention center make every reasonable effort to keep juveniles separate from adults in most activities.[94] It also mandates a classification system that includes separation "and protective custody, where appropriate," of "(1) homosexuals, (2) sexually vulnerable inmates, (3) youthful inmates, (4) inmates vulnerable to assault, (5) inmates incarcerated for the first time, (6) inmates held for trial on minor charges such as traffic violations, (7) mentally ill inmates, and (8) medically ill or defective inmates."[95]

The inmate handbook includes a brief description of the 1993 Revised Consolidated Decree, informing detainees that "Section IX on p. 26 of the Decree designates the Director of Court Compliance and the Inmate Council to monitor the implementation of the Decree. The Inmate Council may have direct access to Plaintiff's counsel for the Decree, Frank M. Danbaugh, Esquire, by telephone weekly."[96] Nevertheless, Danbaugh reported that the Inmate Council had no juvenile representative. "Somebody from the juveniles' section used to come," he said. "But that's no longer permitted because then the juveniles would be mingling with the adults."[97] This practice is in apparent violation of the terms of the consent decree, which describes the Inmate Council as having "representatives from each

---

[93]The 1993 Revised Consolidated Decree defines the plaintiffs in the litigation as "that class of persons, whether men or women, adults or juveniles, pretrial detainees or convicts, who are or who will in the future be confined to the Baltimore City Detention Center." 1993 Revised Consolidated Decree, pp. 4-5. "Juvenile" is defined as "a person under the age of 18 years." Ibid., p. 6.

[94]The decree provides:

> Juvenile residential sections shall only house inmates up to eighteen (18) years of age. No juveniles shall be housed with adult prisoners. Every reasonable effort shall be made to keep juveniles separate from adult prisoners in all activities, except that juvenile and adult inmates may participate together in self-help programs, if their placement is voluntary and is approved by the Warden or designee.

Ibid., p. 12.

[95]Ibid., pp. 11-12.

[96]Division of Pretrial Detention and Services, *Inmate Handbook 1996-1996*, p. 29 (June 1996). The handbook also gives Mr. Danbaugh's address.

[97]Human Rights Watch telephone interview with Frank M. Dunbaugh, May 6, 1998.

unit."[98] As a result, the children detained in the detention center are deprived of the opportunity to participate in one of the chief enforcement mechanisms created by the class action litigation.

The consent decree does not cover the booking and intake center, which houses over 1000 detainees. Because these detainees may remain in the booking and intake center's cells for the duration of their pretrial confinement, the exclusion of the booking and intake center from the consent decree is a significant limitation.[99]

Explaining the state's decision to move to vacate the consent decree, Assistant Attorney General Glenn Marrow told Human Rights Watch in September 1998, "Our position is that the conditions here go well beyond that which is required by the Constitution." He noted that the detention center had recently been reaccredited by the Maryland Commission on Correctional Standards.[100] Later in our interview, however, Commissioner Flanagan told us that he had no serious objection to the consent decree:

> I don't have a problem with the consent decree, and I've operated under it ever since I've been at this detention center. Consent decrees have brought the corrections industry a lot of progress. Without the consent decree in effect at this institution, we would not have seen the progress we've had here in the last fifteen years.[101]

As of October 1999, the court had not yet ruled on the state's motion to vacate the consent decree.[102]

National and Local Standards

The American Correctional Association (ACA) is the leading standard-setting body for juvenile and adult detention and correctional institutions in the United

---

[98]1993 Revised Consolidated Decree, p. 6. In signing the decree, the state "recognized" the "existence and role of the Inmate Council, as representative of the inmates of the Detention Center." Ibid., p. 7.

[99]The booking center is not covered by the consent decree because the decree specifically provides that "[a]ny housing space not described in Appendix B is not part of the Detention Center, and persons detained in housing outside the Detention Center shall not be considered inmates for the purposes of this Decree." Ibid., p. 5.

[100]Human Rights Watch interview with Glenn Marrow, September 23, 1998.

[101]Human Rights Watch interview with LaMont Flanagan, September 23, 1998.

[102]Human Rights Watch telephone interview with Glenn Marrow, October 8, 1999.

States. Compliance with ACA standards is strictly voluntary; facilities apply to the ACA for accreditation and undergo a lengthy application process that includes an on-site review of compliance with the applicable standards. In order to receive accreditation, a facility must demonstrate that it complies with all applicable mandatory ACA standards and at least 90 percent of its nonmandatory standards; the facility may, however, request a waiver for one or more of the standards if it establishes that "overall agency programming compensates for the lack of compliance."[103]

While they represent a positive effort to achieve voluntary compliance with a set of recognized standards, ACA standards do not conform in all respects to international norms. For example, ACA standards for juvenile detention facilities allow the use of isolation for up to five days, but international standards prohibit the use of isolation with children.[104]

In any event, only four of Maryland's twenty-four local jails are accredited by the ACA. The Washington County Detention Center warden commented that the cost of the accreditation process was a barrier to accreditation.[105] In Baltimore, staff explained that the city detention center could not become accredited without significant renovations. "Because of this facility's age, it would have to undergo major reconstruction in order to meet ACA standards. The state won't do it," said Commissioner Flanagan of the Baltimore City Detention Center.[106]

In addition, the National Commission on Correctional Health Care (NCCHC) has released voluntary standards representing minimum requirements for health services in jails and juvenile detention centers.[107] As with ACA standards, compliance with NCCHC standards is voluntary.

Finally, all of Maryland's jails are required to be accredited by the Maryland Commission on Correctional Standards.[108] Although all three sets of standards

---

[103]American Correctional Association, *Standards for Adult Local Detention Facilities,* 3d ed. (Latham, Maryland: ACA, 1991), pp. xvii.

[104]*Compare* American Correctional Association, *Standards for Juvenile Detention Facilities,* 3d ed. (Latham, Maryland: ACA, 1991), p. 67, *with* U.N. Rules for the Protection of Juveniles, Article 67.

[105]Human Rights Watch interview with M. Van Evans, warden, Washington County Detention Center, July 22, 1998.

[106]Human Rights Watch interview with LaMont Flanagan, September 23, 1998.

[107]*See* National Commission on Correctional Health Care, *Standards for Health Services in Jails* (Chicago: NCCHC, 1996); National Commission on Correctional Health Care, *Standards for Health Services in Juvenile Detention and Confinement Facilities* (Chicago: NCCHC, 1995).

[108]Md. Ann. Code, Article 41, § 4-401(b)(7).

generally measure compliance by looking to the existence of written policies, many of the commission's standards fail to offer any guidance on the content of the written policies and procedures. For example, the standard applicable to special confinement merely recites the requirement that "a written policy and procedure" be in place, leaving it to each local detention center to decide what circumstances warrant such placement, how long detainees may be held in special confinement, and what services, activities, and programs detainees will have access to while in special confinement.[109] The few substantive standards offer only minimal protection to detainees.

International Standards

The United States has ratified the two principal international treaties that protect the human rights of detainees: the International Covenant on Civil and Political Rights (ICCPR), ratified in 1992, and the Convention against Torture and Other Cruel, Inhuman or Degrading Treatment or Punishment, ratified in 1994. The United States has also signed the Convention on the Rights of the Child, obligating itself to refrain from acts which would defeat the treaty's object and purpose.[110]

These documents establish that under international law all individuals, whether adults or children, have the right to be free from arbitrary detention and to be protected from cruel, inhuman, or degrading treatment. Article 10(1) of the ICCPR establishes that "all persons deprived of their liberty shall be treated with humanity and with respect for the inherent dignity of the human person," and Article 7 of the ICCPR provides that "[n]o one shall be subjected to torture or to

---

[109] Maryland Commission on Correctional Standards, *Standards Manual: Standards, Compliance Criteria, and Compliance Explanations for Adult Detention Centers* (Baltimore: Commission on Correctional Standards, 1995), Standard ADC.01-P.

[110] International Covenant on Civil and Political Rights (ICCPR), *opened for signature* Dec. 19, 1966, G.A. Res. 2200A (XXI), 999 U.N.T.S. 171 (entered into force Mar. 23, 1976); Convention against Torture and Other Cruel, Inhuman or Degrading Treatment or Punishment, *adopted* December 10, 1984, G.A. Res. 39/46, U.N. Doc. A/RES/39/46, 1465 U.N.T.S. 85 (entered into force June 26, 1987); Convention on the Rights of the Child, *adopted* November 20, 1989, G.A. Res. 44/25, U.N. Doc. A/RES/44/25 (entered into force September 2, 1990). The signatory's obligation not to defeat the object and purpose of a treaty is a recognized principle of customary international law, articulated by the International Court of Justice in a 1951 case and codified in the Vienna Convention on the Law of Treaties. *See* Reservations to the Convention on the Prevention and Punishment of the Crime of Genocide, 1951 I.C.J. 15; Vienna Convention on the Law of Treaties, Article 18(a), 1155 U.N.T.S. 331 (concluded May 23, 1969; entered into force January 27, 1980).

cruel, inhuman or degrading treatment or punishment." Articles 11 and 16(1) of the Convention against Torture obligate the United States to undertake to prevent torture or cruel, inhuman, or degrading treatment while in detention. Article 37(a) of the Convention on the Rights of the Child contains a similar prohibition on torture or other cruel, inhuman, or degrading treatment or punishment.

With respect to children, Articles 10 and 14 of the ICCPR require that detained juveniles be separated from adults and receive treatment appropriate to their age; they also provide that court proceedings involving children "shall be such as will take account of their age and the desirability of promoting their rehabilitation."

The general rules contained in Articles 10 and 14 of the ICCPR are developed more fully in subsequent international documents on children. The Convention on the Rights of the Child recognizes that children are entitled to special care and assistance and that the best interests of the child must be a primary consideration in all actions concerning children. Article 37 of the convention extends specific protections to children deprived of their liberty. Under Article 37:

- no child shall be subjected to cruel, inhuman, or degrading treatment or punishment;
- the arrest and detention of a child must be "used only as a measure of last resort and for the shortest appropriate period of time";
- every child deprived of his or her liberty shall be separated from adults, with the exception of unusual cases in which it is not in the child's best interest to maintain such separation;
- in general, detained children have the right to maintain contact with their family through correspondence and visits;
- every child deprived of his or her liberty shall have the right to "prompt access to legal and other appropriate assistance," the right to "challenge the legality of the deprivation of his or her liberty before a court or other competent, independent and impartial authority," and the right "to a prompt decision on any such action."

Other international standards, notably the U.N. Rules for the Protection of Juveniles Deprived of their Liberty (U.N. Rules for the Protection of Juveniles), the U.N. Guidelines for the Prevention of Juvenile Delinquency (The Riyadh Guidelines), the U.N. Standard Minimum Rules for the Administration of Juvenile Justice, the Standard Minimum Rules for the Treatment of Prisoners (Standard Minimum Rules), and the Body of Principles for the Protection of All Persons under Any Form of Detention or Imprisonment (Body of Principles) provide authoritative guidance for the interpretation of these treaties.[111]

Even when these international standards do not in themselves give rise to rights that are enforceable in U.S. courts, they should be used as aids in interpreting domestic law. The U.S. Supreme Court has recognized, for example, that the Eighth Amendment to the U.S. Constitution "must draw its meaning from the evolving standards of decency that mark the progress of a maturing society."[112] A number of federal courts have cited the Standard Minimum Rules for the Treatment of Prisoners as evidence of contemporary standards of decency.[113] More generally, although the U.S. courts have not traditionally looked at international sources of

---

[111]U.N. Rules for the Protection of Juveniles Deprived of their Liberty (U.N. Rules for the Protection of Juveniles), G.A. Res. 45/113, annex, 45 U.N. GAOR Supp. (No. 49A), p.205, U.N. Doc. A/45/49 (1990); U.N. Guidelines for the Prevention of Juvenile Delinquency (The Riyadh Guidelines), G.A. Res. 45/112, annex, 45 U.N. GAOR Supp. (No. 49A), p. 201, U.N. Doc. A/45/49 (1990); U.N. Standard Minimum Rules for the Administration of Juvenile Justice (the Beijing Rules), G.A. Res. 40/33, annex, 40 U.N. GAOR Supp. (No. 53), p. 207, U.N. Doc. A/40/53 (1985); Standard Minimum Rules for the Treatment of Prisoners, U.N. ECOSOC Res. 663C (XXIV), U.N. Doc. E/3048 (1957), amended by ECOSOC Res. 2076, U.N. Doc. E/5988 (1977); Body of Principles for the Protection of All Persons under Any Form of Detention or Imprisonment (Body of Principles), G.A. Res. 43/173, U.N. Doc. A/43/49 (1988). On the use of these instruments as authoritative guidance for the interpretation of binding treaty standards, see, for example, the U.N. Human Rights Committee's decision in *Mukong v. Cameroon,* citing various violations of the Standard Minimum Rules in ruling that the complaintant was subjected to cruel, inhuman, and degrading treatment. No. 458/1991, U.N. Doc. CCPR/C/51/D/458/1991.

[112]*Trop v. Dulles,* 356 U.S. 86, 101 (1958). The U.S. Supreme Court has "recognized the relevance of the views of the international community in determining whether a punishment is cruel and unusual." *Thompson v. Oklahoma,* 487 U.S. 101, 830 n.31 (1988) (citing *Trop,* 356 U.S. at 102 and n.35; *Coker v. Georgia,* 433 U.S. 583, 596 n.10 (1977); *Enmund v. Florida,* 458 U.S. 781, 796-97 n.22 (1982)). In *Stanford v. Kentucky,* however, the Court "emphasize[d] that it is *American* conceptions of decency that are dispositive, rejecting the contention . . . that the sentencing practices of other countries are relevant." 492 U.S. 361, 370 n.1.

[113]*See Estelle v. Gamble,* 429 U.S. 97, 103-4 & n.8 (1976); *Detainees of Brooklyn House of Detention for Men v. Malcolm,* 520 F.2d 392, 396 (2d Cir. 1975); *Williams v. Coughlin,* 875 F. Supp. 1004, 1013 (W.D.N.Y. 1995); *Lareau v. Manson,* 507 F. Supp. 1177, 1187-89 & n.9 (D. Conn. 1980). In *Lareau,* the federal district court described the Standard Minimum Rules as "an authoritative international statement of basic norms of human dignity and of certain practices which are repugnant to the conscience of mankind." Ibid.

law when deciding cases, individual members of the Supreme Court have indicated a willingness to give weight to the decisions of international tribunals.[114]

U.S. Reservations to International Human Rights Treaties

The United States ratified the ICCPR and the Convention against Torture with several reservations that purport to limit its international law obligations under these treaties. In general, these reservations reflect a unwillingness on the part of the United States to accept a commitment to change existing law or practice. For example, the United States has stated that it considers itself bound by the ICCPR and the Convention against Torture's prohibition on cruel, inhuman, or degrading treatment only to the extent that the Fifth, Eighth, and Fourteenth Amendments to the U.S. Constitution prohibit cruel and unusual treatment or punishment.[115] Additionally, in ratifying the ICCPR, the United States stated that it "reserves the right, in exceptional circumstances, to treat juveniles as adults" for the purposes of sentencing, pretrial detention, and incarceration.[116] Finally, in ratifying both the ICCPR and the Convention against Torture, the United States declared the provisions of each treaty to be "non-self-executing," meaning that individuals cannot rely upon the provisions of these treaties to bring suit in U.S. courts unless the United States enacts enabling legislation.[117] Regardless of whether a treaty is labeled "self-executing," however, the United States is obligated to ensure that it is executed faithfully because the U.S. Constitution provides that international treaties are part of the "supreme Law of the Land."[118]

---

[114]On a tour of European judicial institutions in July 1998, U.S. Supreme Court Justice Sandra Day O'Connor reportedly commented, "'We certainly are going to be more inclined to look at decisions of [the European Court of Justice] on substantive issues . . . and perhaps use them and cite them in future decisions.'" U.S. Supreme Court Justice Stephen Breyer noted, "'Lawyers in America may cite an EU ruling to our court to further a point, and this increases the cross-fertilization of U.S.-EU legal ideas.'" Elizabeth Greathouse, "Justices See Joint Issues with the EU," *Washington Post*, July 9, 1998, p. A24.

[115]*See Multilateral Treaties Deposited with the Secretary-General: Status as at 26 May 1999,* U.N. Doc. ST/LEG/SER.E/, as available on <http://www.un.org/Depts/Treaty> on June 9, 1999.

[116]Ibid.

[117]*See* ibid. The United States attached a total of five reservations, five understandings, and four declarations to the ICCPR. The United States also attached three reservations, five understandings, and two declarations to its ratification of the Convention Against Torture.

[118]United States Constitution, Article VI, clause 2. "Article VI of the [U.S.] Constitution provides expressly for lawmaking by treaty: treaties are declared to be the supreme law of the land. The Framers intended that a treaty should become law ipso facto, when the treaty

Moreover, while international law does permit governments to make reservations to international treaties, such reservations cannot be incompatible with the object and purpose of the treaty.[119] The U.N. Human Rights Committee, which is responsible for interpreting and monitoring compliance with the ICCPR, has stated that reservations or interpretive declarations should not "seek to remove an autonomous meaning to Covenant obligations, by pronouncing them to be identical, or to be accepted only in so far as they are identical, with existing provisions of domestic law."[120]

With regard to Article 7 of the ICCPR, the Human Rights Committee has concluded that "a State may not reserve the right . . . . to subject persons to cruel, inhuman or degrading treatment or punishment,"[121] as the United States purports to do. The United States' reservation to that provision, which would limit the scope of the provision to acts already prohibited by United States law, has been cited as incompatible with the object and purpose of the ICCPR by Denmark, Finland, France, Germany, Italy, the Netherlands, Norway, Portugal, Spain, and Sweden. Incompatible reservations do not invalidate the ratification of a human rights treaty if the ratifying state has indicated its general intent to be bound by the treaty as a whole; instead, the reservation is invalidated.[122] Therefore, Human Rights Watch holds the United States to the full scope of Article 7 of the ICCPR, which provides that no one shall be subjected to torture or to cruel, inhuman, or degrading treatment or punishment.

The Human Rights Committee has also refused to accept reservations which effectively deprive individuals of the means to secure their rights.[123] The United States' declarations that the ICCPR and the Convention against Torture are not self-executing denies individuals the means to obtain a remedy for human rights violations prohibited by these treaties if existing federal or state law does not allow

---

is made; it should not require legislative implementation to convert it into United States law." Louis Henkin, "U.S. Ratification of Human Rights Conventions: The Ghost of Senator Bricker," *American Journal of International Law,* vol. 89 (1995), p. 346.

[119]*See* Vienna Convention on the Law of Treaties, Article 19(3).

[120]U.N. Human Rights Committee, General Comment 24, on Reservations to the ICCPR, para. 19, U.N. Doc. CCPR/C/21/Rev.1/Add.6 (1994). Moreover, international bodies may decline to recognize reservations that are vague or imprecise. *See, for example, Temeltasch v. Switzerland,* App. No. 9116/80, 31 Eur. Comm'n H.R. Dec. & Rep. 138, 145-49 (1983).

[121]U.N. Human Rights Committee, General Comment 24, para. 8.

[122]*See generally* William A. Schabas, "Invalid Reservations to the International Covenant on Civil and Political Rights: Is the United States Still a Party?," *Brooklyn Journal of International Law,* vol. 21 (1995), pp. 277-325.

[123]U.N. Human Rights Committee, General Comment 24, para. 11.

them to challenge these violations. Because these declarations effectively deny individuals access to the courts to secure the rights protected by the ICCPR and the Convention against Torture, they are incompatible with the object and purpose of the treaties.[124]

[124]The United States's statements that it regards these treaties as non-self-executing are evaluated for their compatability with the treaties' object and purpose even though the statements are styled "declarations" rather than "reservations." The U.N. Human Rights Committee has stated, "Regard will be had to the intention of the State, rather than the form of the instrument. If a statement, irrespective of its name or title, purports to exclude or modify the legal effect of a treaty in its application to the State, it constitutes a reservation." Ibid., para. 3.

IV. LIVING CONDITIONS

Children held in Maryland's jails are often placed in overcrowded, sometimes physically deteriorating facilities. Although some jails make efforts to separate juveniles from adults, to some extent children have contact with adult inmates in every detention center visited by Human Rights Watch. In all jails, children complain that they are hungry; one youth in the Baltimore City Detention Center told Human Rights Watch that he avoided exercising out of fear that he would use up needed calories.

Some 150 youth, between one-half and two-thirds of all children held in adult detentions centers in Maryland, are placed in the Baltimore City Detention Center, a crumbling, century-old facility equipped with woefully inadequate light and ventilation and infested with cockroaches and rodents. Maintenance at the jail is irregular. The staff relies heavily on the confinement of detainees to their cells, sometimes for extended periods, as a method of behavior management. As a result, both juvenile and adult detainees must endure appalling conditions of detention.

Girls in adult jails are faced with the prospect of near-total isolation, often left with only each other for company. Human Rights Watch investigators touring Baltimore's jail saw the two girls then in detention standing at the door to their section, their faces pressed to the window and schoolbooks clutched in their arms. When we entered the section, they demanded to know when somebody would come to take them to school, telling us that they had not been to classes for three days. "We thought maybe they forgot about us," one said; they reported that they rarely had contact with guards apart from meals and the times they were taken to and from school.[125]

Conditions in Each Facility

Baltimore City Detention Center

With portions of the Men's Detention Center dating to 1809, Baltimore's city jail is the oldest pretrial facility in use in the state of Maryland. LaMont Flanagan, commissioner of the state Department of Public Safety and Correctional Services's Division of Pretrial Detention and Services, referred to the jail as an "artifact" and described the facility as "your old-style jail that you see on television."[126] An imposing structure in its own right, the jail is adjacent to the Maryland State

---

[125]Human Rights Watch interview, Baltimore City Detention Center, May 11, 1999.

[126]Human Rights Watch interview with LaMont Flanagan, commissioner, Division of Pretrial Detention and Services, Maryland Department of Public Safety and Correctional Services, Baltimore, Maryland, May 11, 1999.

Penitentiary and across the street from the state's new supermaximum security facility.

Approximately 150 juveniles are in detention in the Baltimore City Detention Center on any given day. The vast majority are male, with no more than five to ten girls in detention at one time. (There were only two girls in detention at the time of Human Rights Watch's visit in May 1999.)

Many remain in detention for six months or more. Commissioner Flanagan noted, "According to the statistics, the average stay is seventy-six days. But that's only an average. We have some that stay nine months. Some are up to two years. These juveniles have complicated cases, and they do not plead guilty."[127]

Juvenile defense attorneys confirmed that children tried as adults spend more time in pretrial detention than their counterparts in the juvenile court system and are detained longer than most adult inmates. Attorneys who represent children charged as adults noted that children who face criminal charges have more incentive to contest the charges against them rather than accept a plea bargain. A significant number secure acquittals or dismissal of charges. According to Flanagan, "Fifty percent are released after a prolonged period of time."[128]

Figures reported by the Division of Pretrial Detention and Services demonstrate that juveniles are held in pretrial detention for very long periods. For the period January through October 1996, on average fifty-eight juveniles each month have spent more than three months in pretrial detention. In each of these months, at least two juvenile inmates had been in the detention center for more than one year while awaiting trial; in March 1996, thirty-nine juveniles, 23 percent of the total juvenile population, had spent more than one year in detention pending the resolution of their cases in the circuit or district court.[129]

Male juveniles in the Baltimore City Detention Center are housed in single or double cells in the Men's Detention Center, called the "steel side" by some inmates. Female juveniles are housed in a dormitory in the Women's Detention Center.

---

[127]Human Rights Watch interview with LaMont Flanagan, Commissioner, Division of Pretrial Detention and Services, Maryland Department of Public Safety and Correctional Services, Baltimore, Maryland, May 11, 1999.

[128]Ibid.

[129]Figures are taken from tabular data provided by the Maryland Division of Pretrial Detention and Services to the United States District Court for the District of Maryland, January through October 1996.

The Boys' General Population Section

The general housing area for male juveniles is L Section, located on the second floor of the North Building. Formerly used for inmates on lockup status, the section has a total of sixty cells divided into two sections, each with an upper and a lower tier of fifteen cells each. Bars along the front of each row of cells open onto a passageway; no cell faces any other cell. Exposed pipes, many with torn insulation, line the passageways. The only natural lighting in the section comes from the four or five large windows in each passageway. At the time of our visit in May 1999, most of these windows were partially blocked by plywood or covered by opaque plexiglass or translucent plastic sheeting. Most of the glass panes were broken where the windows were not covered. Each side of the section has two telephones and a dayroom. The single shower room for the section has six shower heads; according to the guards on duty when we toured the section, two shower heads were not working at the time of our visit.

Originally designed for single occupancy, most of the cells in L Section have two bunks and a combination sink and toilet. The majority of the cells measure about eight by seven feet and have eight-and-a-half-foot ceilings; two cells, the first on each side of the upper tier, are slightly larger.[130] The section has two isolation cells with heavy metal sheets completely covering the bars, blocking all natural light from entering the cells. According to the detention center security chief, these cells are not used; he stated that the detention center was in the process of having the metal sheets removed from the bars.[131] We were unable to confirm that no children were held in these cells in L Section.

L Section housed sixty-nine children on the day of our September visit and seventy-one on the day of our May visit. This number is close to the average daily occupancy in the section since the beginning of 1998.[132] Before 1998, the section routinely housed in excess of one hundred, reaching its maximum capacity of 120 in June 1997.[133]

---

[130]*See* 1993 Revised Consolidated Decree, *Duvall v. Schaefer,* Civil Action No. K-76-1255 (D. Md. July 9, 1993), Appendix B., pp. B-1 and B-2.

[131]Human Rights Watch interview with James L. Drewery, security chief, Baltimore City Detention Center, Baltimore, Maryland, May 11, 1999.

[132]On average, the section held approximately sixty-seven juveniles per day between January and September 1998. On February 1, 1999, the section housed sixty-eight juveniles. Maryland Department of Public Safety, Division of Pretrial Detention and Services, Housing Section Reports, January-September 1998, and February 1, 1999.

[133]According to Baltimore City Detention Center housing reports, the section housed 119 juveniles on January 31, 1996; 114 on November 20, 1996; 100 juveniles on June 18, 1997; and 105 on August 1, 1997. Maryland Department of Public Safety, Division of Pretrial

The Girls' Dormitory

Girls are usually housed in Dormitory M in the Women's Detention Center. The dormitory is a large room holding twelve beds. Floor-to-ceiling bars run along the front of the dormitory; one of the other walls has four small windows. The shower and bathroom are at the back of the dormitory. At the time of our visit in May 1999, the shower walls of this dormitory were being stripped of old paint—up to twenty coats, according to our escort—in preparation for refurbishing; during this process, the girls in detention were housed in the girls' protective custody area.

No adults are housed with the juveniles in this dormitory, and detention center officials repeatedly characterized the housing for juveniles as "sight and sound separation" from adults.[134] Nevertheless, women are housed in the next dormitory and could be clearly heard from the girls' dormitory by our researchers. The corrections officer who escorted the Human Rights Watch representatives touring this area conceded, "Well, the female juveniles really can hear the adults. They just can't see them."[135] Even that description was not quite accurate, as girls must walk by three or four adult dormitories, each with floor to ceiling bars along the front, every time they go to or from school, receive visits, take recreation outside their dormitory, or go to the clinic. The officer stated, however, that all adults were locked in their dorms any time a juvenile was in the hallway outside the girls' dormitory.

The Boys' Protective Custody Section

Boys who must be housed separately from the general juvenile population, usually those who are particularly vulnerable or who have been threatened by other juveniles, are placed in protective custody in R Section, on the third floor of the south building. The section housed eleven adults and twenty-six juveniles when we visited in May 1999. Cells in R Section are fifty-three square feet in area, the same size as the regular cells in L Section.[136] They are arranged in a single row of two tiers. Juveniles and adults appeared to be separated; on the day of our May 1999 visit, juveniles were housed in the west wing and adults in the east wing.

Detention and Services, Housing Section Reports, January 1996-August 1997.

[134]For example, Assistant Attorney General Glenn Marrow frequently used this phrase to characterize all juvenile housing areas, repeating it when he accompanied our researchers on a tour of the Women's Detention Center.

[135]Human Rights Watch interview, Baltimore City Detention Center, May 11, 1999.

[136]1993 Revised Consolidated Decree, Appendix B, p. B-3.

Detainees are housed in single cells with bars across the front. Each had an institutional metal toilet and sink and a fluorescent light on the back wall. Cells were dark and bare except for inmates' toiletries and grafitti scrawled on the walls.

The west wing had televisions one-third and two-thirds of the way down the passageway. Raised up on stacked milk crates so that children on both tiers could glimpse a portion of the screen, the sets were tuned to situation comedies.

Standing at the front of their cells, children look through grey bars and past a floor-to-ceiling metal grill separating the upper and lower walkways to their only source of natural lighting, four large windows set in the wall behind the television sets. Ten to twelve feet from the cell doors, these windows are covered with metal grates; as with the windows in L Section, each in this section was also partially blocked by plywood, translucent plexiglass, or opaque plastic sheeting.

The day room has institutional metal tables and stools and was otherwise bare. A dark, filthy shower at the entrance to the west wing had a plastic curtain tied by two corners to a wire across the doorway to the shower.

Protective Custody for Girls

At the time of our May 1999 visit, the girls' protective custody area housed the two girls in the general population while Dormitory M was being refurbished. There were no girls placed on protective custody status at the time of the visit.

Within the section, a series of small single cells, each with a solid metal door fitted with a feeding slot, open onto a passageway. A large fan was placed at one end of the passageway. A minimally furnished dayroom at the other end has two doors with small plexiglass windows. These windows are the only windows in the entire section, meaning that those housed in the section are deprived of natural light altogether. The dayroom has a telephone. A grimy shower is also located in the dayroom, with plastic curtains to afford some small measure of privacy for those using it.

The jail staff has made some effort to compensate for the deficient physical layout of the girls' protective custody section, providing the girls with a television set, a videocassette player, and a cassette tape player. Commissioner Flanagan told us, "The female juveniles have TV sets, video, their own individual Walkmans—they get more because their participation in activities is severely limited. We can't commingle them with the adults."[137] Nevetheless, the two girls in the section described days of unrelieved boredom with few activities.

We also toured the separate adult women's protective custody section in order to see how the Women's Detention Center staff handled a population placed on

[137]Human Rights Watch interview with LaMont Flanagan, September 23, 1998.

protective custody status. Three women were in the dayroom together when we toured the section, which is similar in layout to the girls' protective custody section. The women began to voice their complaints as soon as we entered. "Our main concern is there's no rec. We're in here all day, twenty-four hours a day," said one of the women.[138] Another woman pulled one Human Rights Watch representative aside to substantiate her complaint of close confinement for long hours. Stepping into her cell, she closed the metal door and challenged the researcher to tell her that there was any circulating air coming from the narrow meal slot.

> We're in the cells for ten hours a day from the beginning. There's no way to call the guards if you have a problem. You just have to bang on the door and yell very loudly. They usually let us out into the dayroom at 4:00 but yesterday they forgot or something. I have a medical problem and got sick.[139]

Gesturing at the closed cell door and then back at our representative, who was by this time visibly uncomfortable from the heat and lack of circulation, she continued:

> You see? That's a penalty. You cannot feel any air here. The guards need to come in here. They should bring one more fan at least. I'm not trying to make this a five-star hotel or anything. But we weren't moved to P.C. because we did something wrong. They're supposed to be protecting me. Being in the protecting room doesn't mean you kill me slowly. Ten hours a day in this room with those conditions—we've lost our lives here. We don't go to church or gym. It's crazy. This is like a death penalty prison. It's not like protection.[140]

Boys' Segregation

Boys placed in administrative segregation are housed in M Section. Similar to the protective custody section, this section has the same long tiers of single cells and the same dark and depressing atmosphere. Throughout the section, paint is crumbling from the walls. In an effort to overcome the grafitti and grime, many juveniles had put pictures up on the walls of their cells. In general, the section had

[138]Human Rights Watch interviews, Baltimore City Detention Center, May 11, 1999.
[139]Ibid.
[140]Ibid.

the depressing look of a place in which completely institutionalized individuals knew that they would be spending nearly all of their time.

On the day of our May 1999 visit there were twenty-two juveniles in M Section. No effort was made to place juveniles in a separate wing—their cells were interspersed with those of adult inmates, in violation of international law.[141]

Detainees may be placed on M Section if a disciplinary hearing officer gives them a sanction of a period of administrative segregation after a hearing, if they are awaiting transfer to a state prison after being sentenced to a period of imprisonment of fifteen years or more, or if the warden decides they pose a security risk. Inmates on administrative segregation are allowed two ten-minute showers each week and three one-hour periods of dayroom "recreation" per week. According to James L. Drewery, security officer at the Baltimore City Detention Center, inmates may use the recreation time to watch television or make telephone calls.[142]

Many inmates on M Section are given the additional sanction of "loss of privileges" (LOP), meaning that they are not allowed telephone calls, visits, or commissary privileges for a period that may last the entire time they are placed on administrative segregation. In addition, the juveniles we interviewed told us consistently that they did not receive any recreation periods while they were on LOP.

Two isolation cells are located at the end of the tier. Solid heavy metal sheets placed over the bars shut off virtually all light for anyone inside. Jail officials told us that these cells are used for inmates who have assaulted guards. According to the officers on duty in the section, the inmates housed in these cells receive showers and attorney visits only; they do not receive phone calls, general visits, or any other time outside of their cells. When we inspected the similar isolation cells in L Section, Mr. Drewery told us that no juveniles were held in the cells in that section. No such restriction appears to exist in M Section, however. In February 1999, we interviewed one youth who was housed in one of the isolation cells, albeit at his own request: he told a Human Rights Watch researcher that he had asked to be moved to the isolation cell because the adult inmates in nearby cells continually harassed him by throwing urine and excrement into the cell he originally occupied.[143]

---

[141]*See* ICCPR, Article 10(2)(b); Convention on the Rights of the Child, Article 37(c); U.N. Standard Minimum Rules for the Administration of Juvenile Justice, Article 13.4.

[142]Human Rights Watch interview with James L. Drewery, May 11, 1999.

[143]Human Rights Watch interview, Baltimore City Detention Center, February 9, 1999.

Girls' Segregation

Girls placed in administrative segregation are housed in the women's segregation area, although they do not share cells with women detainees. The section has sixteen cells, each with a single bunk at the back and a combined sink and toilet unit at the front. Each cell has a heavy metal door with small plexiglass windows and a narrow slot for food trays, the only source of fresh air for those inside. The cells had no exterior windows.

When we inspected the showers, we found that one of the two stalls was not functioning and was instead used as a storage area for the cleaning supplies. The other shower was in a vile state, its moldy, torn shower curtain dangling from several hooks. The concrete around the faucets had crumbled away, exposing the piping underneath; we observed cockroaches and other vermin crawling in the cracks.

The guard on duty at the section informed us that detainees on the section are only allowed attorney visits and receive no commissary privileges. Asked how much time each detainee was able to spend outside her cell, the guard replied, "They're outside enough to take a shower and clean their rooms, maybe fifteen to twenty minutes in total. It's two showers a week."[144] Those on "supermax" status—meaning that they spend their entire period of pretrial detention on this section—are allowed outside their cells for a total of one hour each day. The officer told us that supermax detainees may receive visits and make telephone calls. When we pointed out that there was no telephone in the section, our escort explained that inmates could place phone calls through the chaplain's office.

Other Housing Areas

Juveniles are occasionally placed in the psychiatric section, the medical section, and the hospital. In addition, pregnant girls may be placed in the maternity dorm, where a girl was housed as recently as April 1999.

Frederick County Detention Center

With a total inmate population of 339 inmates, the Frederick County Detention Center housed five children at the time of our visit in July 1998. "Our juvenile population is a minimal problem for us," Green said, estimating that the facility took in fewer than fifteen children each year. He told us that the jail has housed children as young as fourteen.[145]

---

[144]Human Rights Watch interview, Baltimore City Detention Center, May 11, 1999.

[145]Human Rights Watch interview with Rob Green, warden, Frederick County Detention Center, Frederick, Maryland, July 21, 1998.

As appears to be the practice in many local detention center with small juvenile populations, Frederick County does not separate children from adult inmates, in violation of international standards.

The facility is modern and clean. The general population areas have two-person cells with an area of approximately seventy square feet and four-person cells with an area of about 120 square feet. The cells are each equipped with a toilet, a sink with hot and cold water taps, and a mirror. All have some natural lighting.

The facility is accredited by the American Correctional Association, the National Commission on Correctional Health Care, the Commission for Law Enforcement Accreditation, and, as required by state law, the Maryland Commission on Correctional Standards. "We're one of thirteen sheriff's offices in the United States to have all possible accreditations," Green noted.[146]

Montgomery County Detention Center

With an average total inmate population of 740, including fifty-eight women, the Montgomery County Detention Center had approximately forty juveniles when we visited in July 1998. At the time of our visit, the youngest inmate was seventeen years old; detention center officials noted that they have had juveniles as young as fourteen in the detention center.

Juveniles are routinely housed in general population areas with adult inmates, although approximately half the juvenile population is placed in the detention center's youthful offender unit. In most living areas, cells are arranged in a circle around a central dayroom. Each of the cells in these areas has two bunks, a toilet, a sink, and a window that allows natural light to enter. In many of the general population units, inmates were out of their cells in the dayroom as we toured the units.

Male inmates under twenty-one years of age are eligible for placement in the youthful offender program if, among other requirements, they are free of infractions for the thirty days prior to entry into the program and have no close relative or codefendant already in the program.[147] This unit has a large dayroom with bright posters on the walls; an educational program was going on as we entered the area.

---

[146] Ibid.

[147] *Handbook for the Youthful Offender Unit of the Montgomery County Detention Center* (Rockville, Maryland: Montgomery County Department of Correction and Rehabilitation, 1998), p. 5.

In sharp contrast to the generally adequate conditions in most of the physical plant, the protective custody unit, built in 1961, is dark and oppressive. The little natural lighting in the section comes from narrow windows in the passage outside the cells. The cells themselves are narrow and grimy, fronted by grey floor-to-ceiling bars. The dayroom is bare except for a few tables and benches bolted to the floor. Lacking virtually any visual stimulation, the unit is a thoroughly depressing place.

The jail is accredited by the American Correctional Association, and officials told us that the facility was found to be 97.2 percent in compliance with all standards when it was evaluated in June 1998. Explaining the facility's failure to achieve full compliance, an official told us, "We didn't achieve 100 percent compliance mostly for construction reasons. We're double-celling, so the number of square feet in each cell is less than ACA standards call for, and there's fewer showers per inmate than ACA standards say there should be. That's all the result of double celling. Another factor is the problem we have with our isolation area. You need to have direct lighting from the cells to the outside, but we have this old construction. These are all problems with the physical plant and the numbers we have here."[148]

Prince George's County Correctional Center

Of the facilities we visited, the Prince George's County Correctional Center is second in size only to Baltimore's city jail. In July 1998, the jail housed 1,350 inmates, including twenty-one children, some as young as fourteen.

Recently reaccredited by the American Correctional Association, the jail was not in complete compliance with the ACA's nonmandatory standards. "Overcrowding," Stanton explained succinctly. "We've got 200 more people than actual rooms. The rated capacity here is 1,140 or 1,150."[149]

Children in the Prince George's County facility are housed in a designated juvenile housing section. Each of the cells in the juvenile section has two bunks, a toilet, sink, mirror, desk, and chair. We saw a television set, a few games, and a number of books in the dayroom.

Washington County Detention Center

Washington County's detention center has an average daily population of 375, approximately 90 percent male. There were eighteen juveniles in detention

---

[148]Human Rights Watch interview, Montgomery County Detention Center, July 30, 1998.

[149]Human Rights Watch interview with Barry L. Stanton, director, Prince George's County Department of Corrections, Upper Marlboro, Maryland, July 23, 1998.

on the day of our visit in July 1998, a number that the warden described as higher than average. Juveniles are routinely commingled with adults.

Originally built to house 140, the jail has increased its capacity by placing multiple bunks in the male general population cells—as many as five bunks in some cells—and by constructing new wings. Most of the male housing sections, known as "pods," have outdoor recreation areas adjacent to the dayrooms; inmates reported that they spent much of their day out of their cells, alleviating some of the discomfort of multiple bunking. Cells in the newest areas of the jail are equipped with desks, and each has a toilet, sink, and a mirror with a shelf above the sink. The newer cells have windows which the inmates can open to allow a measure of fresh air to enter.

At the time of our July 1998 visit, the jail was in the process of renovating a minimum security area in order to improve housing conditions for the female inmates. A guard explained that the women's housing unit was designed to hold thirty detainees; in recent years, the jail has had to find housing for as many as sixty or seventy. "We've realized that we cannot continue to pack these women upstairs like sardines," the guard told us.[150]

Separation from Adults

We found that children were commingled with adults to some degree in all of the detention centers we visited, in clear violation of international law.[151] In the smaller jails, no effort was made to house children apart from adult inmates; in many cases, juveniles shared cells with adults in these jails. In the larger facilities, all of which had separate housing areas for the juveniles in the general population, we nevertheless found that children placed on administrative segregation were routinely housed in close proximity to adults. In addition, we found that in nearly all facilities juveniles are commingled with adults when placed in protective custody or in medical and psychiatric areas.

In Baltimore, children housed in the general population and protective custody sections were generally kept separate from adult inmates. We found that this was not true in the segregation, medical, and psychiatric sections of the jail. "It's juveniles throughout," said an officer assigned to the segregation section, meaning that juveniles were interspersed with adults throughout the section. He gave one of our researchers a list of the numbered cells which housed juveniles,

---

[150]Human Rights Watch interview, Washington County Detention Center, July 22, 1998.

[151]*See* ICCPR, Article 10(2)(b); Convention on the Rights of the Child, Article 37(c). *See also* U.N. Standard Minimum Rules for the Administration of Juvenile Justice, Article 13.4; U.N. Rules for the Protection of Juveniles, Article 29.

allowing us to verify that youth were housed alongside adults. We did not find any instances of children sharing cells with adults, however.

We found the same to be true of Baltimore's psychiatric section. Although Commissioner Flanagan told us, "We have never used E Section for juveniles,"[152] a Human Rights Watch representative interviewed a child in that section several hours later. Indeed, a review of the jail's daily population records from 1995 to 1999 revealed that juveniles were routinely housed with adults in the section, albeit in small numbers.

Similarly, jail officials accompanying us through the Women's Detention Center in Baltimore initially told us that girls were never housed in the women's segregation section, and indeed none were housed in the section on the day of our visit. Several months prior to our May 1999 visit, however, a Human Rights Watch researcher interviewed a girl who said that she was one of four juveniles placed in the women's segregation section.[153] The officer on duty in the women's segregation section at the time of our visit confirmed that the section had routinely housed juvenile inmates. "A couple of months ago I had five at once, I think it was February," she said. Flipping through her log book, she confirmed that six juveniles had been placed in the women's segregation section in February 1999, four for twenty-day periods and two for thirty days each.[154]

Furthermore, girls who are pregnant may be housed with adults in the Women's Detention Center maternity dormitory. "We have had one juvenile in here," a guard told us. "It required the approval of the commissioner and the warden. That was about a month ago. She was here with the adults, but she could not rec [take recreation] with the adults, only with the other juveniles."[155]

In Montgomery County, approximately twenty juveniles were housed in general population units, sometimes sharing cells with adults. Thomas C. spent two weeks in a Montgomery County general population unit when he first arrived at the age of sixteen. He reported that he was housed with inmates of all ages, sixteen to sixty. "The only reason I felt comfortable was because my co-defendant was in the same dorm." David L., sixteen, had been in four general population wings at the time of our interview. In one wing, he found out that some of the older inmates were planning to "jump" him; the shift counselor moved him to a different wing after his cellmate wrote a letter to the unit guards. Alex S., age sixteen, agreed that the Montgomery County general population unit where he was

---

[152]Human Rights Watch interview with LaMont Flanagan, May 11, 1998.

[153]Human Rights Watch interview, Baltimore City Detention Center, February 10, 1999.

[154]Human Rights Watch interview, Baltimore City Detention Center, May 11, 1999.

[155]Human Rights Watch interview, Baltimore City Detention Center, May 11, 1999.

held for three weeks was "kind of an experience," because of the wide range in ages, but told us that he never had a problem with the adult inmates.[156]

Although the director of the Prince George's County Correctional Center told us, "We separate the juveniles by sight and sound even though they're waived to adult status,"[157] we found that strict separation was not always enforced. When we toured the juvenile housing area, we learned that up to forty adults were housed at times on bunks in the juvenile section's dayroom. Detention center officials explained that this arrangement was occasionally required because of the level of overcrowding at the facility. When adults are bunked in the juvenile dayroom, they must lie on their bunks without talking during the times when the children use the dayroom; in turn, the juveniles are locked in their cells during times that the adults are allowed to use the dayroom.

In the smaller jails we visited, we found that it was the norm to commingle juveniles and adults. Frederick County does not separate juveniles from adults as a matter of routine, although the detention center's director noted that individual juveniles will be moved out of the general population if they are thought to be at risk.[158] Similarly, we found that juveniles are routinely commingled with adults in the Washington County Detention Center. "The officers may attempt to separate the juveniles from the adults, but it's not done as a matter of procedure. They're treated as adults," explained Washington County's warden.[159]

Light, Ventilation, and Temperature

Most of the facilities we visited house juveniles (and all other inmates) in cells with adequate lighting, including direct access to natural light, consistent with international standards.[160] In all housing areas of the Baltimore City Detention Center and in the protective custody section of the Montgomery County Detention Center, however, inmates have no windows in their cells. For many, the only sources of natural light are the windows across the hall from their cells, although we saw a good many windows that were obscured by grime, constructed of opaque materials, or covered altogether. Some isolation cells in Baltimore's detention

---

[156]Human Rights Watch interviews, Montgomery County Detention Center, July 30, 1998.
[157]Human Rights Watch interview with Barry L. Stanton, July 23, 1998.
[158]Human Rights Watch interview with Rob Green, July 21, 1998.
[159]Human Rights Watch interview with M. Van Evans, warden, Washington County Detention Center, Hagerstown, Maryland, July 22, 1998.
[160]Article 11 of the Standard Minimum Rules calls, "[i]n all places where prisoners are required live or work," for windows "large enough to enable the prisoners to read or work by natural light."

center were almost entirely covered by metal sheets so that almost no natural light reached the cells. There are no outside windows whatsoever in the girls' protective custody and segregation areas in the Baltimore City Detention Center.

We repeatedly heard complaints about ventilation and temperature from children held at the Baltimore City Detention Center. "It's hot right now," said Evan M., held in Baltimore. "But in the winter it's always cold. We have blankets but it's still cold because the windows are busted out." Carl A. agreed. "It's hot. Too hot," he said. "Sometimes they give fans to whoever's been here the longest, but there are only two fans."[161] Marlow P., another Baltimore detainee, explained, "How it's feeling outside is how it's feeling here."[162]

Clothing

Children at all facilities we visited were required to wear institutional uniforms. Most of the facilities we visited issued children grey, green, or orange jumpsuits. In Baltimore, children were given surplus camouflage army issue; adult inmates at the facility were not required to wear uniforms.

While the practice of requiring detainees to wear uniforms is not uncommon in many adult pretrial detention facilities in the United States, it is not the rule in the overwhelming majority of juvenile facilties across the country. Indeed, international standards call upon institutions to allow juveniles and pretrial detainees to wear their own clothing.[163]

We observed that the youth in the Baltimore City Detention Center could wear their personal clothing in their cells; according to corrections officials, children are only required to wear the uniforms outside their cells. Youth seemed to dislike the uniforms, probably in part because they are uncomfortably warm, and we did not see any wearing the uniforms inside their cells. The jail is not air conditioned and was already very warm when we visited in May 1999, particularly on the upper tiers. The heavy uniforms appeared to be unsuitable for the hot summer months from June through August, in contravention of international

---

[161]Human Rights Watch interviews, Baltimore City Detention Center, July 17, 1998.

[162]Human Rights Watch interview, Baltimore City Detention Center, May 11, 1999.

[163]Article 36 of the U.N. Rules for the Protection of Juveniles states: "To the extent possible juveniles should have the right to use their own clothing." Similarly, international standards emphasize that pretrial detainees, who benefit from the presumption of innocence, "shall be allowed to wear [their] own clothing if it is clean and suitable." U.N. Standard Minimum Rules for the Treatment of Prisoners, Article 88(1).

standards that "[d]etention facilities should ensure that each juvenile has person clothing suitable to the climate."[164]

Children at other jails also commented that they preferred to wear their own clothing. Bruce W., held in Montgomery County, remarked, "A lot of us order sweats, t-shirts, boxers, and stuff. Mostly we don't wear our greys [the color of the uniform in Montgomery's Youthful Offender Unit], only during groups. When we're on our own time, we wear our own clothes."[165]

James L. Drewery, Baltimore's security chief, told us that children could either send their personal clothing to the laundry or give it to their families to get it washed. Recently, however, many children have had difficulty getting clothing to and from family members because their section has been on lockdown for extended periods of time since November 1998. Brad D., a seventeen-year-old who entered the jail in April 1999 during a time when the section was locked down, told us that he went two weeks without a change of underwear because his mother had not been able to bring him clean clothes until several days before our May visit:

> I had to wear the same drawers two weeks straight. They didn't let my mother drop off clean drawers or socks for me. It don't make no sense. I don't know why they didn't let her bring them, I guess because we on lockdown. She visited me last Saturday and gave me three pairs of boxers and three pairs of socks. That the first time she was able to visit since I been here.[166]

When asked how they had their clothes cleaned, several children said that they would not get their clothes back if they sent them to the laundry. Consequently, they wash their clothing in the toilet in their room with liquid hand soap.

We heard a number of complaints from children held at the Baltimore City Detention Center that their court clothes, stored in lockers at the entrance to each section, were often dirty when they were retrieved in preparation for court dates. "They only let us have one court outfit," Jerome T. said. "They put them in these unsanitary lockers. Mice be pissing on your clothes."[167]

Jail staff across Maryland cited security as the reason for requiring juveniles to wear uniforms. Since youth in most juvenile facilities wear ordinary clothing

---

[164]U.N. Rules for the Protection of Juveniles, Article 36.
[165]Human Rights Watch interview, Montgomery County Detention Center, July 30, 1998.
[166]Human Rights Watch interview, Baltimore City Detention Center, May 11, 1999.
[167]Human Rights Watch interview, Baltimore City Detention Center, May 11, 1999.

such as t-shirts and shorts or pants, there is a real question whether there is an actual security justification for the uniforms. In the absence of actual incidents of violence directly related to clothing or a similar justification, the validity of requiring youth to wear stigmatizing, institutionalizing, and often uncomfortable clothing is questionable.[168] In Baltimore, the fact that adult inmates are not required to wear such uniforms casts further doubt on the security rationale advanced by jail officials.

Bedding

With the notable exception of the Baltimore City Detention Center, the bedding provided in the jails we visited appeared to be in compliance with international standards requiring that each child "be provided with separate and sufficient bedding, which should be clean when issued, kept in good order, and changed often enough to ensure cleanliness."[169] Many children in Baltimore complained to us that their mattresses were dirty, thin, and inadequate. Showing us grimy foam pads or filthy cloth pallets with little padding, they clearly felt humiliated to be forced to sleep on the mattresses they were issued.

We also heard several complaints that the Baltimore detention center did not provide clean sheets frequently enough. Although jail staff told us that sheets were laundered every week, we heard from some children that their sheets were washed every two weeks or even less frequently.

A number of juveniles in the city detention center told us that they had blankets stolen from their cells. For example, Josh S., a seventeen-year-old held in L Section, told us that when he returned from court the previous week, he discovered that not only his blanket but also his mattress was gone. When he asked for a new mattress, he was given an old cloth ticking covered with plastic.[170] Particularly during the winter months, the theft of blankets may be due in part to the lack of adequate heating and the fact that many window panes are broken during the hot summer months and never repaired.

Hygiene

Most of the jails visited by Human Rights Watch were reasonably clean and offered inmates daily access to showers. Many of the children expressed satisfaction to us when this subject came up. "They let you shower every night,"

---

[168] *See* U.N. Rules for the Protection of Juveniles, Article 36 (noting that clothing "should in no manner be degrading or humiliating").

[169] Ibid., Article 33.

[170] Human Rights Watch interview, Baltimore City Detention Center, May 11, 1999.

Bruce W. said of Montgomery County's Youthful Offender Unit. "It's the policy here. That's one of the good rules—you have to practice good hygiene." William M. added, "You can shower any time during the day except when they have the count. It's required at least once a day." He stated that those in the unit always had the opportunity to shower after the gym or outside recreation.[171]

Again, the notable exception was the Baltimore City Detention Center. Our representatives saw cockroaches crawling across the floor on the day of our visit, and we heard repeated complaints that the jail was infested with mice and other vermin. "There's roaches. Sometimes you see rats running up around the lights," Evan M. told us. Carl A. echoed these complaints, reporting, "I see cockroaches and mice every day."[172] A number of detainees told us that when they were given their court clothes, which were stored in lockers at the front of each section, they found that their clothing was stained and covered with mouse droppings.

While such problems are due in part to the age of the Baltimore detention center's physical plant, they are compounded by an evident lack of maintenance. In each section, we saw windows covered with plywood, plexiglass, and plastic sheeting; many window panes had been smashed out and simply not replaced. Cells were grimy; detainees pointed out brown stains and residue that had been on the walls since they arrived.

"How I gonna keep my cell clean?" asked an adult detainee in the segregation section. "I don't have a broom. They tell us to clean but they don't give us stuff to clean with." In an effort to keep his cell as tidy as possible, he finally asked an detainee worker to give him some scouring powder and a rag. Another detainee reported that he used an old toothbrush and water from his sink to scrub down his walls and floor.[173]

Except when they were on lockdown, children held in Baltimore's general juvenile population section reported that they were given a chance to take a shower every day or at least every other day. In some sections, however, many of the shower nozzles were broken; Alex S., interviewed in July 1998, reported that four of the seven showers in his section were not working. Carl A. told us, "You can shower as long as you want to until the next side gets the showers. That's thirty minutes. But there's no showers if we get locked down."[174]

Because of the frequency and length of lockdowns imposed at the jail after November 1998, we heard very different accounts from children in L Section

---

[171]Human Rights Watch interviews, Montgomery County Detention Center, July 30, 1998.
[172]Human Rights Watch interviews, Baltimore City Detention Center, July 17, 1998.
[173]Human Rights Watch interviews, Baltimore City Detention Center, May 11, 1999.
[174]Human Rights Watch interviews, Baltimore City Detention Center, July 17, 1998.

interviewed after that date. Paul G., interviewed in February 1999, said, "The top tier hasn't been in the shower since Sunday night," three nights before. "We're supposed to shower every day. The jail was on MSC [master security check] last night, I don't know why, so we didn't get a shower. We didn't get no showers on Monday either. They didn't tell us why."[175]

Those placed in segregation are permitted only two ten-minute showers each week. Jackson F., held in segregation for a week during the summer, told Human Rights Watch, "The cell is so hot all you think about is a shower. You deal with it by taking a 'birdbath.' That's where you wash from the sink in your cell. You do that every day, all day long, wash up every three hours or so."[176]

Baltimore's restrictions on showers run counter to the National Commission on Correctional Health Care standard, which calls for daily opportunity to bathe.[177]

All of the jails we visited ensured that indigent inmates received basic toiletries. Indeed, the Baltimore City Detention Center is required under the terms of the 1993 revised consent decree to provide indigent inmates with toothpaste, a toothbrush, clean clothing, and shaving supplies.[178] The children with whom we spoke confirmed that indigent inmates received a "welfare kit" containing these items.

We heard one further complaint regarding hygiene from virtually all of the children we interviewed at the Baltimore City Detention Center after November 1998, when the detention center began to be locked down on a regular basis. During lockdown periods, inmates are usually not permitted to order items from the commissary except for the supplies they would receive if they were indigent. Children complained that this practice prevented them from obtaining items they considered necessary, such as skin lotion and oil for their hair. Two told us that they felt that they had developed skin conditions as a result. Even if there were some valid penological reason for restricting commissary purchases during lockdown periods—and it is not clear that such a restriction serves any purpose other than punishment—there is no reason why children should be prohibited from purchasing basic toiletries with their own money. Skin lotion and hair oil can readily be added to the list of items that may be purchased from the commissary

---

[175]Human Rights Watch interview, Baltimore City Detention Center, February 10, 1999.
[176]Human Rights Watch interview, Baltimore, Maryland, March 9, 1999.
[177]National Commission on Correctional Health Care, *Standards for Health Services in Jails* (Chicago: NCCHC, 1996), p. 59.
[178]*See also Duvall v. Shaefer,* Civil Action No. K-76-1255, 1988 U.S. Dist. LEXIS 18298, *20 (D. Md. Aug. 30, 1988).

items during lockdown; the jail should immediately remove its restrictions on these items.

Food

> *Seems like we don't eat enough here. I get three trays a day, but the hours are so awkward, the portions so small, it's not enough. After 4:00, you hungry, with no snack or nothing. Being as you in jail, you don't expect too much, but you expect them to keep you full. I've lost twelve pounds since I got here—my mother noticed it. It's not because I'm not eating. I don't miss a meal. It's not enough food.*
>
> —Michael T., detained for six months in Prince George's County while awaiting trial

"The most frequent complaint on food is quantity—they want more," a Baltimore City Detention Center official told Human Rights Watch at a meeting.[179] That statement proved to be true for all of the facilities we visited. While a number of children characterized the quality of the food they received as "poor" or complained that "some days it's just not cooked," Human Rights Watch researchers heard complaints about the size of meal portions with disturbing frequency.

At every facility where we conducted interviews, children told us that their meals left them feeling hungry. Carl A., in Baltimore, commented, "It's not enough food. We need at least another tray."[180] Peter B., detained in Washington County, told us, "I've been in juvenile. You get more there. They have to give you so many calories. It's not enough here."[181] "No, you don't get a lot to eat here," Bruce W. told us during an interview at the Montgomery County Detention Center.[182] Alex S., in Baltimore, said, "It's not enough food. I'd want a whole bunch more than I get now."[183] Paul G., another Baltimore detainee, replied to our question about the food by stating, "Not enough for me. Not enough at all meals, really."[184]

Children at the Prince George's County Correctional Center told us that early meal hours were the reason that they were often hungry in the evenings. They receive breakfast at 4:00 a.m., lunch at about 10:00 a.m., and dinner by 5:00

---

[179]Human Rights Watch interview with LaMont Flanagan, September 23, 1998.
[180]Human Rights Watch interview, Baltimore City Detention Center, July 17, 1998.
[181]Human Rights Watch interviews, Washington County Detention Center, July 22, 1998.
[182]Human Rights Watch interview, Montgomery County Detention Center, July 30, 1998.
[183]Human Rights Watch interview, Baltimore City Detention Center, July 17, 1998.
[184]Human Rights Watch interview, Baltimore City Detention Center, February 10, 1999.

p.m.[185] "You get pretty hungry in between," Nestor S. told us, "and what they bring is not enough. No seconds." Other children held in Prince George's County echoed these concerns. "It's not enough food," said Diane S., who told us that she had been given a tray with raw meat once. "It don't fill us up, but we get to order from the commissary," said Jermaine C. When asked what he would change about the food, Brian W. immediately replied, "Bigger portions."[186]

At all institutions we visited, children reported that most inmates were not allowed to have seconds. "You get that one tray," Jenile L. said of Prince George's County. Michael T., also in Prince George's County, reported that those who worked on kitchen detail did receive seconds, a privilege that was denied to the general population.[187]

In the absence of sufficient food during regular meals, children supplement their meals with food purchased from the commissary. "I eat my commissary. It's not really enough, but you don't have no choice," Jenile L. told us. "I order commissary—noodles and things, but it's a lot less than I need. I want a lot more," said Evan M., held in the Baltimore City Detention Center.

In fact, many children reported that commissary food formed an essential part of their diet. Ron P., a Washington County inmate, said the amount of food he was able to eat was "only enough if you buy commissary. What they give you, they don't give you hardly anything."[188] William M., in Montgomery County, told us that meal portions were only "enough because we order from the canteen."[189] Asked what kinds of food he bought to supplement the regular meals, Paul G. recited a list that included noodles, potato chips, pretzels, peanuts, candy, and cookies.[190]

---

[185]Maryland standards require that meals be "ample in portion" and "served at reasonable intervals." The standards call for "[t]hree distinct meals during each 24-hour period, two of which ought to be hot," and "served to ensure that an interval of not more than 14 hours is maintained between the evening meals and breakfast." Maryland Commission on Correctional Standards, *Standards, Compliance Criteria, and Compliance Explanations for Adult Detention Centers,* p. 38 (1991). *Accord* American Correctional Association, *Standards for Adult Local Detention Facilities,* 3d ed., p. 84 (Latham, Maryland: ACA, 1991) (calling for "at least three meals (including two hot meals) . . . provided at regular meal times during each 24-hour period, with no more than 14 hours between the evening meal and breakfast").

[186]Human Rights Watch interviews, P.G. County Correctional Center, July 23, 1998.

[187]Human Rights Watch interviews, P.G. County Correctional Center, July 23, 1998.

[188]Human Rights Watch interview, Washington County Detention Center, July 22, 1998.

[189]Human Rights Watch interview, Montgomery County Detention Center, July 30, 1998.

[190]Human Rights Watch interview, Baltimore City Detention Center, February 10, 1999.

Most of the children interviewed at the Baltimore City Detention Center mentioned that they bought dried noodles, which, according to the cooking directions, are made by adding boiling water. "What's amazing to me is that they sell this food that you need hot water to prepare," recounted a former detainee. Some children used hot water directly from the tap in a utility closet, when they are able to have a guard open it for them. Others described elaborate means by which they actually cooked the food in their cells: After making a "doughnut" by tightly wrapping up toilet paper or strips torn off a sheet, inmates light it by making a spark from a wall socket and then use the flame to boil water for the noodles. "You take a tissue and stick a piece of lead on the end," explained Jackson F.. "But you can't hold it to the socket too long or you short out the circuit. If that happens, you get in trouble with the guys with TVs—they get mad at you because they can't watch their TVs."[191]

Those who can't afford commissary items go hungry unless they are able to get commissary items from others. "If somebody don't eat something, you can give them a cup of soup or chips from the commissary, or you trade the things you don't eat," explained Sam H., in the Washington County Detention Center.[192] Often, children told us, they lose their commissary items to theft or coercion. "Some folks here, I've never seen order commissary," Michael T. observed, "but then I see them with commissary stuff."[193]

The U.N. Rules for the Protection of Juveniles Deprived of their Liberty provide that youth in detention must receive food at normal meal times and of a quality and quantity to satisfy the standards of health and hygiene.[194] Youth

---

[191]Human Rights Watch interview, Baltimore, Maryland, April 9, 1999.

[192]Human Rights Watch interview, Washington County Detention Center, July 22, 1998.

[193]Human Rights Watch interview, P.G. County Correctional Center, July 23, 1998.

[194]U.N. Rules for the Protection of Juveniles, Article 37. The federal district court in Maryland has noted that "[b]ad quality of prison food and the lack of appropriate dietary balance can add up to a level of constitutional deficiency." *Collins v. Schoonfield,* 344 F. Supp. 257, 278 (D. Md. 1972) (citing *Landman v. Royster,* 333 F. Supp. 621, 647 (E.D. Va. 1971); *Holt v. Sarver,* 309 F. Supp. 362 (E.D. Ark. 1970)). Furthermore, the Baltimore City Detention Center's failure to provide adequate meals is a violation of 1993 consent decree, which requires that "[e]ach inmate shall have the opportunity to have three (3) appropriate meals daily, served in a palatable manner. The diet shall consist of food of adequate nutritional value." 1993 Revised Consolidated Decree, p. 17. The 1988 decree specified that meals would include "(1) fruit juice or fresh fruit on a daily basis; and (2) fresh milk (offered as a beverage) at least three (3) meals weekly," 1988 Revised Consolidated Decree, 1988 U.S. Dist. LEXIS 18298, *20-21, but that requirement was not carried over to the 1993 version.

corrections specialists concur that children need more food than adults do. "Young people require at least 3,000 calories per day, including frequent opportunities to eat, both meals and snacks," writes Barry Glick, a corrections consultant and former associate deputy director for local services with the New York State Division for Youth.[195] The National Commission on Correctional Health Care estimate is even higher—up to 4,000 calories per day or more for teenagers who are still growing or very active.[196]

Our impression that officials at adult jails did not understand the dietary needs of their juvenile inmates was confirmed when an official at the Baltimore City Detention Center told us during a meeting of detention center staff that the facility served its inmates "2,200 to 2,800 calories per day, depending on the population. The NCCH standard is at 1,800; others are 2,000 calories. We're well within the dietary requirements. That's not unusual in any correctional setting." Asked about children in detention, he replied, "The juveniles would get that higher caloric intake because of their needs."[197] However, he was not able to explain how the meals served to juveniles differed from those offered to adults. Indeed, the meals we saw served to juveniles appeared to be identical to those offered to adults—the portions served to juveniles appeared to consist of the same items, to be the same size, and served on trays that were not marked to distinguish them from the meals offered to adult inmates.

---

[195]Barry Glick, "Kids in Adult Correctional Systems," *Corrections Today*, August 1998, p. 99.

[196]National Commission on Correctional Health Care, *Standards for Health Services in Juvenile Detention and Confinement Facilities*, Appendix E, p. 116 (Chicago: National Commission on Correctional Health Care, 1995). The juvenile health standards note that "[t]he amounts and types of foods suggested . . . will satisfy the needs of most teenagers. However, those who are still growing or are very active will require increased portion sizes, primarily of grain and milk products, as well as fruits and vegetables." Ibid.

The commission's standards for adult jails do not directly address the dietary needs of adolescents, but they call for "an adequate diet supplied to all inmates that incorporates the principles expressed in the United States Department of Agriculture/Department of Health and Human Services (USDA/DHHS) Food Guide Pyramid meeting the current recommended Dietary Allowances *for appropriate age groups.*" National Commission on Correctional Health Care, *Standards for Health Services in Jails,* p.57 (Chicago: National Commission on Correctional Health Care, 1996) (emphasis added).

[197]Human Rights Watch interview, Baltimore City Detention Center, September 23, 1998.

V. JUVENILE-ON-JUVENILE VIOLENCE

In all facilities, juveniles reported that they had been subjected to harassment and violence from other detainees. In some cases, children housed with adults reported that they had been targeted by the adult detainees; many others stated that they felt unsafe being around the adults. Violent incidents among detainees are particularly serious in the Baltimore City Detention Center. Because of the facility's age, detainees are readily able to fashion handmade weapons, known as "shanks." In an effort to prevent juveniles from bringing weapons onto L Section, jail guards thoroughly search children on their way to and from school, usually conducting a strip search when the children return from classes.

Most disturbingly, we heard a number of reports that guards in the Baltimore City Detention Center occasionally permitted juveniles to fight each other. According to these reports, guards permit such fights, called "square dances" because they take place in an open square area on the upper tier, apparently in the belief that they allow youths to settle scores without risking a general mêlée.

Harassment and Violence

Children at all of the jails we visited reported that harassment and violence from both juvenile and adult detainees was a regular occurrence. Joey N., seventeen, described the exceptionally degrading harassment he endured from the adult inmates in the segregation section of the Baltimore City Detention Center:

> My first cell had kind of a grill where the door was. Every day, the other inmates, they would throw stuff at me. You know, like shit and stuff. I complained to the C.O.'s, but they didn't do nothing. I can't count the number of times I asked the C.O.'s to move me. I said, "Can you move my cell?" They said no, but they seen the shit. Every day I'm getting shit thrown on me from the other cells. I didn't want to say nothing out loud directly, because the other guys would just keep doing it. I just kept asking to get moved.

In desperation, he resorted to telling the guards that he was suicidal so that he would be moved to a special area for those on suicide watch. "I just wanted to get out of that cell," he said. When he was discharged from the mental health unit and returned to M Section, he requested to be placed in one of the section's isolation cells in an effort to avoid having excrement thrown into his cell:

> If you put a sheet on the grill, they tell you to take it down. I asked to go in this cell, they call it the dungeon. Dungeon's the one got a steel

> door. Ain't nothing in it, just a toilet and a bed. I'm the only person in there. I stay there twenty-four hours a day, only come out Tuesday and Friday for a five-minute shower, then get locked back in.[198]

Most often, we heard accounts of fights between youths. "Always going to be fights," said Darryl S., a seventeen-year-old detainee in Baltimore.[199] Asked about the frequency of fights between inmates at the Washington County Detention Center, Ron P., sixteen, replied, "Probably once or twice a week. Nobody ever gets caught. Ain't nobody gonna snitch." He described a fight that had broken out the previous week: "It's going on about ten minutes, and the C.O.s ain't catching them. I guess they just weren't paying attention. The one guy, he could really have gotten hurt if some of us didn't stop it."[200] Nestor S., detained in Prince George's County, explained, "I'm from Southeast, see. Say there's another guy from Northeast. We don't get along. We're going to have to meet up sometime."[201]

In Montgomery County's Youthful Offender Unit, Bruce W., age seventeen, told us that there was a lot of "play fighting" in the cells:

> It's like you really fighting but at the end you still friends. You be trying to see which one is harder. Mostly everybody thinks they the baddest one because it's no horseplay outside the cell. The cell is the only place to do it. It happens every night. You can hear it, the sound of fists hitting raw skin. You be slamming up against the wall. You can't make a lot of noise because then you get sent to the holding cell.[202]

Asked whether the juveniles were injured in these "play fights," he described bruises and scars from hitting up against the walls, bunks, and toilet.[203]

Jenile L. reported frequent fights in the women's area of the Prince George's County Detention Center, although she noted that the situation had improved at the time of our interview in July 1998. "A lot of the instigators are gone now," she said. "The last fight was a week, maybe a week and a half ago." Asked what the female detainees fought about, she answered, "It's a lot of things. It might be

---

[198]Human Rights Watch interview, Baltimorew City Detention Center, February 9, 1999.
[199]Human Rights Watch interview, Baltimore City Detention Center, May 11, 1999.
[200]Human Rights Watch interview, Washington County Detention Center, July 22, 1998.
[201]Human Rights Watch interview, P.G. County Correctional Center, July 23, 1998.
[202]Human Rights Watch interview, Montgomery County Detention Center, July 30, 1998.
[203]Ibid.

because somebody steal something. Or maybe you just don't like somebody. Or it might be over one of those males."[204]

We were unable to conduct interviews of children in Frederick County. Asked about incidents of detainee violence in the jail, the warden stated that he knew of few instances but readily conceded that detainees were unwilling to report incidents of violence to jail staff. "The inmate code contaminates our ability to know much about inmate-on-inmate violence," he said.[205]

We heard the largest number of reports of violence and harassment from children held at the Baltimore City Detention Center. When we asked an official about juvenile-on-juvenile violence in the jail, he said, "There's something maybe once, twice a week. It's difficult to assess unless they tell us they have an enemy."[206] During our May 1999 visit to the jail, we reviewed all special incident reports involving juveniles that had been filed within the previous nine months. The reports documented a total of thirty-five incidents: twelve assaults or stabbings, eleven shakedowns or threats of violence, two instances in which youth threw urine or feces, four fights between youth, four incidents in which shanks were found, and two fires on the tiers.

With incidents of violence occurring at an average of one per week in a population of about 150 youth, the number and frequency of incidents raise concerns about the safety of youth (and staff—in January 1996, two juvenile detainees reportedly assaulted a security officer, stabbing him in the back of the neck with a metal shank).[207] The use of lengthy periods of cell confinement and the paucity of programming and other activities may be major contributing factors to this high level of violence. Put another way, improvements to the physical surroundings and an increase in the amount of education and other programming may significantly reduce these incidents.

Even if improvements along these lines are made, they will not change the fact that the jail as a whole is a very dangerous place. Between mid-1995 and early 1999, the detention center reported an average of eighty-one detainee assaults on

[204]Human Rights Watch interview, P.G. County Correctional Center, July 23, 1998.
[205]Human Rights Watch interview with Rob Green, warden, Frederick County Detention Center, Frederick, Maryland, July 21, 1998.
[206]Human Rights Watch interview, Baltimore City Detention Center, September 23, 1998.
[207]*See* Peter Hermann, "Stabbing, Gun Prompt City Jail Lockdown; 100 Weapons Are Found in Detention Center Search," *The Baltimore Sun,* January 20, 1996, p. 16B.

inmates involving the use of a weapon per year and some 865 assaults not involving a weapon each year.[208]

Availability of Weapons

Children at the Baltimore City Detention Center consistently recounted a widespread incidence of weapons among the juveniles on L Section. Joey N., seventeen, told Human Rights Watch that juveniles regularly carried knives during the three months that he was housed on L Section:

> Sometimes it's real knives, sometimes they make knives. Sometimes they get kitchen knives. The whole section has knives. People got to keep them for a reason, because they fear for their life. If you feel you're gonna get stabbed up and the C.O.'s not gonna do nothing, you got to take matters into your own hands.[209]

"Yeah, there's knives," confirmed Maurice B., fifteen. "They make them."[210] Jackson F. explained that the juveniles pulled off parts of the vents in the school, made of four temporary structures put together:

> If you look at the floors of the cells, you can see where they're smooth from sharpening the metal. You learn the technique of putting water down over the floor first—that way it doesn't leave scraping marks.[211]

"There were a lot of other places" where inmates could get metal to make knives, he told us. "Some guys took the long screws off of the basketball hoops. Some other folks got into a room in the courtyard where they store the weights." He told us that most often, the juveniles obtained knives from the adult inmates. "Sure, we're supposed to be separated from the adults. But we go to court with adults, we see them in the bullpens, they're in the yards, they're in the infirmary, we see them on the way to school, we see them in the visiting room." Juveniles may arrange for workers to deliver knives or other contraband. "Somebody puts

---

[208] *See* Maryland Department of Public Safety and Correctional Services, Division of Pretrial Detention and Services, *Violence Reduction Program* (Baltimore, Maryland: BCDC, 1999), pp. 15-16.
[209] Human Rights Watch interview, Baltimore City Detention Center, February 9, 1999.
[210] Human Rights Watch interview, Baltimore City Detention Center, February 10, 1999.
[211] Human Rights Watch interview, Baltimore, Maryland, April 9, 1999.

it on a lunchtray. Then you tell the feedup guy, 'Make sure sixty-eight gets this tray.'"[212]

Several youths recounted their first-hand experiences with shanks. "One boy put a knife in me, but it wasn't sharp enough" to draw blood, Sam H. told us, saying that he himself used to have a knife and "was about to use it" on another juvenile before it was confiscated. "I wanted his tennies," he explained, referring to the other inmate's shoes. "He wouldn't cooperate."[213] Others readily admitted to owning or using knives. "If you stab someone up, you don't have to worry about anyone messing with you," said Shawn G., repeating later, "If you try to kill someone, put a shank in their neck, you're all right."[214]

From July 1998 to March 1999, the detention center reported that seventy-two detainee assaults on other detainees involved the use of weapons. In March 1999, the jail confiscated 108 weapons during searches of the facility.[215] In a news account published in November 1997, a Baltimore detainee estimated that at least one-third of the detainees in the detention center and the booking center had homemade metal shanks.[216] Commissioner Flanagan attributed the prevalence of weapons to the age of the jail, saying, "If we didn't have this dilapidated structure, violence would be a nonissue."[217]

The "Square Dance"

Human Rights Watch researchers heard several accounts that guards allowed youths to fight with each other. "That's the square dance," Jackson F. explained. "There's a little area on the tier by the phones," about eight feet by eight feet. "The guards will lock everybody in their cells except for two guys" who begin to fight.[218]

"Someone calls you up," Sam H. told us. "If you have something on your chest, you can do it in front of the police," presumably referring to the correctional officers, "or you can do it somewhere else. I prefer to do it somewhere else." He

[212]Ibid.

[213]Human Rights Watch interview, Baltimore City Detention Center, May 11, 1999.

[214]Human Rights Watch interview, Baltimore City Detention Center, May 11, 1999.

[215]*See* Maryland Department of Public Safety and Correctional Services, Division of Pretrial Detention and Services, Baltimore City Detention Center, *Violence Reduction Program* (Baltimore: BCDC, 1999), pp. 13-14.

[216]*See* Ivan Penn, "Lethal Handiwork Behind Prison Walls; Search for Shanks Never Turns up All," *The Baltimore Sun,* Nov. 17, 1997, p. 1A.

[217]Human Rights Watch interview with LaMont Flanagan, commissioner, Division of Pretrial Detention and Services, Maryland Department of Public Safety and Correctional Services, Baltimore, Maryland, May 11, 1999.

[218]Human Rights Watch interview, Baltimore, Maryland, March 9, 1999.

claimed that the officers had recently started giving inmates boxing gloves to use during the square dance, a development which he felt made the fight less satisfying. "You ain't getting what you want off your chest," he commented.[219]

Jackson F. described a square dance:

> You've got your peekers out. There's a lot of yelling from everybody, but if it gets too loud the officers will tell you you need to be quiet or they'll break up the dance. It ends up with busted heads, slashes over your eyes, broken fingers, cut lips, maybe a broken nose. But you don't go to the hospital for the cuts. If you did, there'd have to be a report, and the guards would have to explain why two guys were out in the square while everybody else was locked in.[220]

Other juveniles in L Section corroborated these accounts. "C.O.'s let you go in the square and get it off your chest," said Darryl S., volunteering that the guards provided boxing gloves. Shawn G., who told us that he had seen square dances twice, said that they began with a shakedown by guards to ensure that the participants had no weapons. In one of the fights, which took place about a month before our interview in May 1999, a juvenile suffered a split lip that could have gotten infected. He stated that the boy should have gotten stitches for the injury but instead received only an ice pack; the swelling took a week to go down. When he was asked why the boy did not receive medical attention, Shawn G. replied that if the guards took the juvenile off the section they would have to explain what happened.[221]

Asked why the corrections officers would permit two youths to fight, most children speculated that guards preferred to have fighting occur under somewhat controlled conditions instead of risking larger conflicts. "Figure would rather let you fight than have someone getting stabbed up. It's better than C.O.'s don't know what's going on and leads to someone getting stabbed up," said Shawn G.[222]

---

[219]Human Rights Watch interview, Baltimore City Detention Center, May 11, 1999.
[220]Human Rights Watch interview, Baltimore, Maryland, March 9, 1999.
[221]Human Rights Watch interviews, Baltimore City Detention Center, May 11, 1999.
[222]Ibid.

VI. DISCIPLINE

Particularly in the Baltimore City Detention Center, we heard frequent complaints from children that they were punished arbitrarily or excessively. Our review of disciplinary records in that jail found many instances in which children were given lengthy periods of segregation, often with loss of visits and other privileges, for relatively minor offenses. In many more serious cases, we were concerned to find that disciplinary hearing officers routinely gave juveniles the maximum sanction possible, ninety days in segregation per charge, and in some cases directed youth to serve their sanctions consecutively.

Also in Baltimore, we found that the jail frequently locked down entire sections, sometimes the entire facility, for days or even weeks after an escape or fight. When such measures do not serve an immediate security rationale, they amount to punishment and may violate international law and the U.S. Constitution. Moreover, such extended lockdowns constitute collective punishments, explicitly forbidden by international standards.[223]

In all facilities, specialized training is needed: offered at regular intervals, such training would enable corrections officers to tailor their behavior management techniques to adolescents and might well reduce the number of disciplinary offenses involving juveniles.

Notice of the Rules

As a preliminary matter, we found that many children reported that they had never seen a copy of their institution's rules; those who had received printed copies could not explain most of the rules in their own words.[224] Ron P., sixteen, told us that he had never seen a copy of the Washington County Detention Center's rules.

---

[223]Pretrial detainees, presumed innocent until proven guilty, must be accorded "separate treatment appropriate to their status as unconvicted persons." ICCPR, Article 10(2)(a). Under U.S. law, a pretrial detainee may not be confined under conditions that "amount to punishment." *Bell v. Wolfish,* 441 U.S. 520 (1979). Article 67 of the U.N. Rules for the Protection of Juveniles calls for a prohibition on the use of collective sanctions.

[224]International standards require that children be given a copy of the institution's rules upon admission. *See* U.N. Rules for the Protection of Juveniles, Article 24. Further, "[a]ll juveniles should be helped to understand the regulations governing the internal organization of the facility, the goals and methodology of the care provided, the disciplinary requirements and procedures, other authorized methods of seeking information and of making complaints and all such other matters as are necessary to enable them to understand fully their rights and obligations during detention." Ibid., Article 25. *See also* Standard Minimum Rules, Article 35.

"You're supposed to get a handbook, but I didn't get one. I just asked questions. You learn from other people's mistakes, too." When we asked him how he knew about the handbook, he replied, "Everybody else had one. I asked them about getting one, and they said they'd get back to me, but they never did. Now I've just been here long enough to know the rules."[225]

In Montgomery County, however, William M., age sixteen, told us that he was given an orientation by the counselors when he entered the Youthful Offender Unit. "The rules are on the wall, too, right over there," he added, pointing.[226]

Our discussions with officials at the Baltimore City Detention Center raised questions about the adequacy of the notice of the offenses with which youth may be charged and the sanctions that these offenses may carry. James L. Drewery, the security chief for the Baltimore City Detention Center, told our researchers that the list of offenses and sanctions was "in the library" and that youth "have access" to it.[227] In fact, the only list the jail staff was able to show our researchers was on the back of the administrative segregation charging form; that list included all offenses but did not give the possible sanctions for each. Moreover, the general population had been on lockdown for much of the six months preceding our May 1999 visit. Most of the children with whom our researchers spoke told us that they had never been to the library; the few who had been there stated that they had not gone to the library in a very long time.[228] Even if children had "access" to the library, as Mr. Drewery asserted, the placement of a list somewhere in the library hardly constitutes fair notice of particular offenses and possible sanctions.

In addition, several of the violations at the Baltimore City Detention Center are vague, allowing the hearing officer enormous discretion to decide whether the inmate is guilty. The classification of seriousness of other offenses appears to be arbitrary. Fred Nastri, one of fifteen hearing officers for the state of Maryland, told us, for example, that "masturbation" and "indecent exposure" are Category One offenses, grouped with offenses such as assault and battery on staff or the use of a weapon.[229] Neither offense seems especially serious, certainly not on par with

---

[225]Human Rights Watch interview, Washington County Detention Center, July 22, 1998.

[226]Human Rights Watch interview, Montgomery County Detention Center, July 30, 1998.

[227]Human Rights Watch interview with James L. Drewery, security chief, Baltimore City Detention Center, Baltimore, Maryland, May 11, 1999.

[228]*See* Part X, "Contacts with the Outside World, "Access to the Library" section.

[229]Violations are classified into one of four categories. Category One contains the most serious offenses, such as assault or battery on staff or the use of weapons. Drug offenses, Category Two offenses, include the hoarding of medications. Category Three offenses include contraband, disrespect, and being "out of bounds." Category Four offenses are

assault or weapons charges. Drug offenses, listed in Category Two, and possession of contraband, Category Three, would appear to be much more dangerous.

Disciplinary Hearings

Fred Nastri told us that disciplinary hearings are held regularly and that inmates brought up on disciplinary charges ("ticketed") are entitled to have an inmate represent them and may call witnesses. According to Nastri, all of the hearing officers have at least undergraduate degrees and ten of the fifteen officers have master's degrees.[230] Our review of the files of all children held in administrative segregration found that the hearing officers' decisions are actively reviewed by an administrator at the facility. In some cases, the review overturned the hearing officer's decision.

Despite these positive aspects of the disciplinary process, we noted several serious concerns. Once children are charged, hearing officers have a great deal of discretion to impose long terms of disciplinary segregation, up to ninety days for a single violation. Mr. Nastri told us that hearing officers apply sanctions by following written sentencing guidelines. He was not able to produce a copy of these guidelines, however. In addition, although he described himself as a "very experienced" hearing officer, he could not tell us how much time would be the standard sanction for a fight between youth, a threat made to a guard, or other specific examples we offered him.[231] His inability to answer such questions suggested that no clear guidelines exist and that the sanction is left completely to the discretion of the hearing officer.

When we asked children what sanctions they might expect for various offenses, they nearly always replied that they could expect to receive thirty to ninety days of lockup. While some raised specific instances of punishment that they considered unfair, others expressed their approval of the discipline imposed by the hearing officers. Paul G., a fifteen-year-old on L Section, told us, "You get sent to lockdown for knives, fighting, disrespecting the C.O. or the teacher. You get any amount of days the hearing officer give you. I think that's good what they be doing. Seems like everybody trying to get away with stuff."[232]

Mr. Nastri told us that he may impose "informal" dispositions outside the formal hearing process. The sanctions imposed through the informal process are

---

violations of the technical institutional rules and regulations. Human Rights Watch interview with Fred Nastri, hearing officer, Baltimore City Detention Center, May 11, 1999.

[230]Ibid.

[231]Ibid.

[232]Human Rights Watch interview, Baltimore City Detention Center, February 10, 1999.

less severe than those which may be imposed in a formal disciplinary hearing. Mr. Nastri stated, for example, that he might allow a youth to stay in general population with a thirty-day restriction on commissary or visits. While he implied that a substantial portion of the misconduct by youth is handled through informal dispositions, our review of special incident reports for the six-month period ending in May 1999 found few written records of informal dispositions.[233]

At least for those in the formal hearing process, it appears that some period of segregation is the standard response to disciplinary offenses rather than the last resort in a graduated tier of sanctions. The failure to consider alternatives runs counter to accepted penal practice. ACA standards permit the use of disciplinary segregation "only after an impartial hearing has determined (1) that other available alternative dispositions are inadequate to regulate the inmate's behavior within acceptable limits and (2) that the inmate's presence in the general inmate population poses a serious threat to the orderly operation or security of the facility."[234]

A related concern is raised by the additional measures that hearing officers often impose on those found guilty of disciplinary offenses. In addition to the ninety days of cell time per charge, sanctions can include loss of phone calls, loss of visits, loss of commissary privileges, or the loss of all of those together (known as "loss of privileges" or LOP). Inmates given loss of privileges receive only two ten-minute showers each week and, at least in theory, are given only one hour outside their cell for "recreation" three times per week. The imposition of loss of privileges or some of these individual measures may be abusive in themselves. For example, in those instances where the loss of phone calls and visits denies children contact with their family members, the use of such sanctions violates international standards.[235] Particularly when these additional measures are combined with lengthy periods of administrative detention, as they often are, the total sanction may be very broad and potentially quite punitive.

When a youth is charged with a disciplinary violation, he or she may be held on lockdown for three to five days while awaiting a disciplinary hearing. Mr. Nastri told us that the hearing officers may dismiss the disciplinary charges if the juvenile does not receive a hearing within five days, but he stated that hearing

---

[233]Human Rights Watch interview with Fred Nastri, May 11, 1999.

[234]American Correctional Association, *Standards for Adult Local Detention Facilities,* 3d ed. (Lanham, Maryland: ACA, 1991), p. 67.

[235]"[T]he restriction or denial of contact with family members should be prohibited for any purpose." U.N. Rules for the Protection of Juveniles, Article 67.

officers will not do so unless the child raises the issue.[236] It is unrealistic to expect that an unrepresented juvenile detainee would be aware that disciplinary charges may be dismissed for this reason.

Disciplinary Segregation

We reviewed the files of all twenty-two juveniles held in segregation on the day of our March 1999 visit to the Baltimore City Detention Center. Two had been given ninety days' segregation with loss of privileges for stabbing other youth; one of the two received an additional ninety days with loss of privileges for having a shank in the gym. Nine were in administrative segregation for having shanks or other weapons, generally receiving thirty to forty-five days and loss of privileges.[237] These periods of disciplinary segregation are in addition to any criminal penalties the children might receive—all of those serving segregation time were waiting for criminal charges to be filed for the assaults or weapons charges.

We were concerned to find that a substantial number of youth received the maximum ninety days per charge and some juveniles were sentenced to serve their sanctions consecutively—sentenced to ninety days each for two charges brought simultaneously, these children were segregated for a total of 180 days. Even for cases in which some period of confinement would be appropriate, such lengthy periods of segregation are far in excess of those recommended by the American Correctional Association. The ACA standards applicable to juvenile detention facilities call for no more than five days of such confinement.[238] Even for adults, these periods of segregation are excessive. ACA standards applicable to adult jails call for a sixty-day maximum on disciplinary segregation imposed for all violations arising out of one incident, and they provide: "Continuous confinement for more than thirty days requires the review and approval of the facility administrator."[239]

In calling for a significantly shorter maximum period of isolation for detainees in juvenile detention centers, the ACA standards reflect the view of psychiatrists that extended cell confinement has grave consequences for an adolescent's mental health. For example, one psychiatrist specializing in child and adolescent psychiatry provided testimony in federal district court that

---

[236]Human Rights Watch interview with Fred Nastri, May 11, 1999.

[237]Of these nine youth, several had prior weapons possession offenses and received longer segregation periods with exended periods of loss of privileges. For example, one juvenile received 195 days of loss of privileges; another lost privileges for 180 days.

[238]American Correctional Association, *Standards for Juvenile Detention Facilities,* 3d ed. (Laurel, Maryland: ACA, 1991), p. 67.

[239]American Correctional Association, *Standards for Adult Local Detention Facilities,* p. 68.

> extended isolation of a youngster exposes him to conditions equivalent to "sensory deprivation." This is a state of affairs which will cause a normal adult to begin experiencing psychotic-like symptoms, and will push a troubled person in the direction of serious emotional illness.
>
> What is true in this case for adults is of even greater concern with children and adolescents. Youngsters are in general more vulnerable to emotional pressures than mature adults; isolation is a condition of extraordinarily severe psychic stress; the resultant impact on the mental health of the individual exposed to such stress will always be serious, and can occasionally be disastrous.[240]

Moreover, not all youth were placed in segregation for such serious misconduct. Some were confined for long periods for behavior that was considerably less dangerous. Three children were charged with fighting with other youth and refusing to stop when ordered by guards to do so. One youth threatened another for his sweat pants and received ninety days of segregation with loss of privileges. Another youth received forty-five days after throwing a bar of soap at a guard and telling him to get off the tier. A third received sixty days with loss of privileges after refusing to go into his cell when ordered and reportedly becoming belligerent toward the staff. In each of these instances, the written report suggested that disputes between juveniles or between juveniles and staff escalated into physical confrontations. In many juvenile facilities, fights of this type would be answered by a brief period of cell confinement to allow the youths to calm down; an important part of the sanction would be to find out the basis for the dispute between the juveniles and attempt to resolve it. In these cases, however, the juveniles involved in two of the incidents received thirty days in segregation with loss of privileges; a third was given ninety days with loss of privileges.

Children held at the Baltimore City Detention Center frequently complained that they were punished arbitrarily or excessively. TerenceB., a seventeen-year-old in segregration, told us that his time on that status had been extended for an extra ninety days as punishment for throwing trash into the hallway so that it could be swept up, something that he said the juveniles in L Section were routinely told to do. "I didn't know that could get me ninety days on lockup," he said, shaking his head. "I didn't know the rules were different on M Section."[241]

---

240 *Lollis v. New York State Department of Social Services,* 322 F. Supp. 473, 481 (S.D.N.Y. 1970) (quoting affidavit of Joseph D. Noshpitz, M.D.).

241 Human Rights Watch interview, Baltimore City Detention Center, April 30, 1999.

The imposition of long periods of cell confinement in such cases is excessive and punitive when applied to juveniles, particularly when lengthy confinement is accompanied by loss of privileges. Such treatment may amount to violations of constitutional rights and international standards.[242]

"Supermax"

In the Baltimore City Detention Center, juveniles may be placed on "supermax," meaning that they are housed in administrative segregation for their entire period of pretrial detention. According to Mr. Drewery, the warden may order a juvenile placed on administrative segregation without a hearing, based solely on his review of the youth's record.[243] The warden's decision to assign juveniles to administrative segregation does not appear to be based on verifiable factors such as prior misbehavior; instead, the disciplinary reports frequently contain only a notation that jail staff suspected that the youth posed a safety risk.

Juveniles and other detainees placed in administrative segregation have no regular means of obtaining review of this decision. Commissioner Flanagan told Human Rights Watch that juveniles placed on administrative segregation "are told why they are reclassified"; according to him, many youths write letters to the warden asking him to review their placement. Nevertheless, he conceded that the detention center had not established an appeal process to review supermax placements: "You're right. They can write to the warden, but I won't sit here and tell you that there's an adjudicatory process."[244]

While there is no question that jail authorities have the ability to deal with detainees who pose security risks, the process described by Commissioner Flanagan and Mr. Drewery raises fundamental due process concerns. Under the system in effect in Baltimore, a youth who has not been convicted of a crime may

---

[242]International standards prohibit the use of "closed or solitary confinement or any other punishment that may compromise the physical or mental health of the juvenile concerned." U.N. Rules for the Protection of Juveniles, Article 67. In the United States, courts have found constitutional violations where a fourteen-year-old was isolated for two weeks with no recreation and no access to reading materials, in the case of a juvenile placed in isolation for seven days and shackled for part of that time, and where youth were punished by being placed in isolation rooms for up to twenty-four hours. *See* Lollis, 322 F. Supp. at 482; *H.C. v. Jarrard,* 786 F.2d 1080, 1087-88 (11th Cir. 1986); *Milonas v. Williams,* 691 F.2d 931, 941-42 (10th Cir. 1982).

[243]Human Rights Watch interview with James L. Drewery, May 11, 1999.

[244]Human Rights Watch interview with LaMont Flanagan, commissioner, Division of Pretrial Detention and Services, Maryland Department of Public Safety and Correctional Services, Baltimore, Maryland, May 11, 1999.

be placed into virtually unlimited administrative segregation—approximately twenty-three hours of oppressive cell confinement each day—without a hearing and without committing any offense while in the jail.

Use of General Lockdowns

We heard frequent reports during our interviews that juveniles in the Men's Detention Center of the Baltimore City Detention Center are often placed on lockdown, meaning that they are restricted to their cells with limited or no access to showers, recreation, visitation, religious services, and education. Usually imposed on detainees throughout the men's facility in response to a fight or a discovery of contraband, lockdowns can last a month or more.

"We go on lock a lot," reported Paul G. in February 1999. "Can't come out your cell, no showers, no phone calls. The only ones who can come out is the working men."[245] While he told us that the juveniles on the section are able to go to school and are sometimes given access to the gym during these periods, they are not allowed into the dayroom and are not given library privileges.

The Baltimore City Detention Center was locked down in its entirety from November 1 to November 9, 1998, in response to a stabbing which occurred in T Section on October 30, 1998. In explanation, the state assistant attorney general assigned to the detention center wrote, "Whenever there is a homicide within the Division's facilities, the Division routinely locks down for a number of reasons. These reasons include, but are not limited to: (1) the initiation of any criminal or administrative investigation to the causes of the homicide; and (2) the initiation of a mass contraband search of the entire facility."[246]

Subsequently, an escape from the detention center on November 27, 1998, resulted in a forty-two-day general lockdown from the end of November 1998 to the second week in January 1999. The assistant attorney general justified this response by noting that "the Division initiated a criminal and administrative investigation as to the cause of the escape," that "there was a mass search for contraband in the entire facility," and that because "there were many potential security breaches in MDC [the Men's Detention Center] . . . . MDC was locked down until physical repairs could be made to eliminate these potential problems."[247]

---

[245]Human Rights Watch interview, Baltimore City Detention Center, February 10, 1999.

[246]Letter from Glenn T. Marrow, assistant attorney general, to Frank Dunbaugh, February 3, 1999, p. 1.

[247]Ibid., pp. 1-2

Commissioner Flanagan repeated that explanation during our May 1999 visit to the jail.[248]

According to the policies of the Division of Pretrial Detention and Services, inmates are allowed visits only by legal counsel and clergy during lockdown periods; "all other visits, recreation, and library privileges are suspended" and "phased in when appropriate." Detainees were reportedly allowed holiday visits from December 28, 1998, to January 1, 1999, but could not make phone calls to notify their families that the restriction on visitation had been temporarily lifted.[249]

James L. Drewery, the detention center's security chief, explained to Human Rights Watch that the commissioner "gave the juveniles the opportunity to earn their rights back with their behavior in school. The juveniles have earned their rights back to visits, and they just earned their rights back to commissary."[250]

The application of broad restrictions to the entire male facility for lengthy periods of time appears at best to be arbitrary, lacking any valid security rationale; at worst, such a response is intended to punish rather than ensure safety. The comments of Commissioner Flanagan and his staff strongly suggest the latter. Such collective punitive measures are prohibited under international standards.[251]

Abuses by Guards

We heard few reports of abuses by guards; most children interviewed reported that they felt comfortable around the corrections officers. "They look out for us, especially the evening officer," remarked Anthony P. of the Prince George's County guards. Jenile L., fifteen, told us that while some Prince George's County guards "will cuss at you," others were nice; she had never seen physical violence by the staff.[252] Dylan C., in the Baltimore City Detention Center, commented, "I

[248]Human Rights Watch interview with LaMont Flanagan, May 11, 1999.

[249]Marrow letter, p. 2. In response, the inmates' attorney in the class action litigation wrote to Assistant Attorney General Glenn Marrow that "with the telephones turned off, they could only advise their families by letter, but no mail was scheduled to go out until 12/28. What sadist suggested this cruel Christmas amnesty?" Letter from Frank M. Dunbaugh to Glenn Marrow, assistant attorney general, December 29, 1998, p.1.

[250]Human Rights Watch interview with James L. Drewery, May 11, 1999.

[251]*See* U.N. Rules for the Protection of Juveniles, Article 67. While we heard accounts of group punishments at other jails, none applied such punishments with the severity or the regularity we heard of in Baltimore. For example, Bruce W. described a common instance of group accontability in Mongomery County, telling us, "If it's loud up here, the whole dorm gets locked in. If it's loud by the phone areas, the whole dorm gets locked in." Human Rights Watch interview, Montgomery County Detention Center, July 30, 1998.

[252]Human Rights Watch interviews, P.G. County Correctional Center, July 23, 1998.

like the C.O.'s here. They do a good job. They respect us, we respect them." Similarly, Sam H. characterized most of the Baltimore guards as "cool" but added, "Certain ones want to act smart. They only do it because we're young."[253]

When we did hear reports of abuses by staff, the juveniles' accounts revealed a common pattern in which guards, provoked by adolescent insolence, react with violence to reassert their authority. Terence B., a seventeen-year-old in the Baltimore City Detention Center's segregation section, told Human Rights Watch that a guard pushed him face-first into his cell door while he was handcuffed. Explaining that the entire section had been handcuffed during a weapons search, he told us,

> I was standing outside my cell with the cuffs on my wrists. All of a sudden this C.O. comes up and yells, "Get your ass back inside!," and started to push me back in my cell. I told him wasn't no need to grab me. Then he pushed me hard into the cell door. I raised my hand up so I wouldn't hit my face against the door, and I bounced back away from the door. He slammed me down on the ground and hit me in the face a couple of times. A few other C.O.'s jumped on me then. Then that first C.O. wrote me a ticket. He claimed I was resisting him and pushing him.[254]

At his disciplinary hearing, the hearing officer saw that his jail-issue fatigues were ripped. "He asked me how they got ripped, and I told him it happened during the shakedown when the C.O. banked me." Based on Terence B.'s testimony and inconsistencies in the officer's written report, the hearing officer dismissed the disciplinary charges.[255]

Michelle R., also in Baltimore, told Human Rights Watch,

> I've been beat up by one C.O. but not a lot. It was when there was a fight in the dorm. This one officer, he don't like us, always be calling us out. One time I told him if he can't respect me, don't say nothing. So that fight, it was at night, on the eleven to seven a.m. shift. When he came up to break it up, he threw me to the wall. I tried to tell him I wasn't going to do nothing, but he pushed me down against the bed. Then he threw me up against the wall and choked me. That was the first

---

[253]Human Rights Watch interviews, Baltimore City Detention Center, May 11, 1999.
[254]Human Rights Watch interview, Baltimore City Detention Center, April 30, 1999.
[255]Ibid.

> of this month. I got somebody to tell my sister. I snuck to the phone when we took our showers. My sister and mother talked to him. He said he didn't do nothing. I told the assistant warden. I haven't heard anything, but he hasn't worked then, not on this side, not that I know of.
>
> Another time, I saw a C.O. hit another girl. It was a while ago, in October I think. She got smart with one of the C.O.'s, so the C.O. got mad and slapped her. They just wrote her a ticket to put her on lock. They be lying on her like that, sent her down on lock. I don't know if she complained. That's what happens—C.O.'s will tell you if you wise up that it don't matter, they'll put you where you supposed to be.[256]

James S., in the Montgomery County Detention Center, stated,

> What they try to do, they aggravate you to where you do something, then they lock you down. They get power through the situation. They do things to make you get mad, but after you do something you learn you didn't get nowhere. Just 'cause they got power, that's what they do. Like, one time, the C.O.'s did something to this inmate, and the dude tried to stab at them with a pen. All the C.O.'s came in and beat up the dude. The dude's head get busted. Wasn't nothing done to the C.O.'s. Fair and equal treatment don't happen.[257]

The Need for Specialized Training

International standards recommend that the personnel of a detention facility should receive regular training to enable them to carry out their duties effectively.[258] In the case of corrections officers working at adult detention centers, such training is critical to enable them to interact effectively with juvenile detainees. The Montgomery County Detention Center's Youthful Offender Quality Action Team has found, for example:

> Behavior management methods effective with adults (21 years of age and older) incarcerated at the Montgomery County Department of Correction and Rehabilitation do not seem to be effective when used with the youthful offender (under the age of 21 years). This is

[256]Human Rights Watch interview, Baltimore City Detention Center, February 10, 1999.
[257]Human Rights Watch interview, Montgomery County Detention Center, July 30, 1998.
[258]*See* U.N. Rules for the Protection of Juveniles, Article 85.

> demonstrated by the increasing number of disciplinary incidents incurred by the youthful offender. Although in 1995 (up to the date of the study) youthful offenders made up 12.6% of the detention center population, they accounted for 23.2% of the disciplinary infractions.[259]

These data suggest that specialized training may be far more successful in reducing disciplinary incidents than the approach currently employed in Baltimore, the imposition on the entire section of extended cell confinement with complete loss of privileges. In Baltimore and in all other adult jails in which children are detained, jail administrators should seek to provide their staff with training provided by professionals who specialize in the care and custody of juveniles.

The Baltimore City Detention Center has already taken a related step that may have an effect on the incidence of infractions among the juvenile population. Organizing corrections officers in teams, James L. Drewery, the detention center's security chief, has given groups of officers greater responsibility within the security structure.[260] These teams of officers may be more likely to take a greater interest in the populations under their custody. Baltimore can build on this initiative by designating a team of officers to oversee the juvenile population and providing the officers with specialized training in the developmental and other issues specific to working with this population.

---

[259]Renee N. Parcover, "The Youthful Offender Quality Action Team's Final Report," p. 2 (Rockville, Md.: Montgomery County Department of Correction and Rehabilition, n.d.).
[260]Human Rights Watch interview with James L. Drewery, May 11, 1999.

VII. MEDICAL AND MENTAL HEALTH SERVICES

Every facility we visited offered basic medical services to detainees, and children at all facilities reported that they had received some sort of examination by medical staff shortly after their arrival. However, children frequently complained that they would have to wait a week or more to see a nurse or doctor if they became sick after receiving their initial medical examination; some youth reported that their requests for medical assistance were ignored altogether.

In at least one facility, we learned that medical staff did not regularly offer gynecological examinations, providing them to girls and women only upon request. Additionally, we learned that not all jails have separate medical facilities for female detainees, particularly for those on suicide watch. In the Washington County Detention Center, we saw an adult woman placed on observation in a cell at the front of the booking and intake section, in full view of the male guards and detainees who regularly passed by.

In Maryland and across the United States, detainees have a higher incidence of mental illness than the population as a whole. Accordingly, mental health services are a critical aspect of medical care in jails. In our tour of Baltimore's detention center, where Human Rights Watch's investigative team included a mental health professional, we were disturbed to find serious deficiencies in the mental health program.

General Medical Care

All of the jails Human Rights Watch visited had procedures in place to examine detainees upon their admission. All of the children we interviewed reported that they were screened by medical staff within several days of their arrival.

Nevertheless, children frequently told us that they had difficulty seeing medical staff when they were sick or needed dental care. "You got to write a lot of times," said Joey N., held in the Baltimore City Detention Center.[261] Marlow P., a sixteen-year-old in Baltimore, told us, "I put out a sick call, but not been called yet. That was three weeks ago."[262]

"The amount of time it takes to see inmates depends," Montgomery County medical staff told Human Rights Watch. "It could be six days unless it's an emergency." Thomas C., a Montgomery County detainee, told us that he had made five requests to see the doctor during the nineteen months he had been at the jail;

---

[261] Human Rights Watch interview, Baltimore City Detention Center, February 9, 1999.
[262] Human Rights Watch interview, Baltimore City Detention Center, May 11, 1999.

it usually took two weeks before he would be seen. He reported that another inmate contracted appendicitis but said that the corrections officer did not take the inmate seriously. Eventually, he told us, the inmate had to be taken out of the unit on a stretcher.[263]

Michelle R., a fifteen-year-old in Prince George's County, estimated that it takes a week or more to be seen after filling out a sick call slip. She stated that when she had an earache, it took six days before she saw the doctor. In addition, at the time of our interview in July 1998 she had been waiting for one week to see the dentist for a toothache. Jenile L. stated, "I've been waiting to go to the dentist. It says in the handbook that we can get temporary fillings. Mine fell out two and a half months ago. They not called me yet. I keep putting in requests for the dentist. It's ten or more slips I've put in." Similarly, Nestor S. told us that he had asked to see a doctor after becoming sick. "They told me, 'okay,' but never got around to seeing me." However, Michael T., another Prince George's County inmate, reported that his cellmate saw the doctor four or five hours after putting in his request. "He has sickle cell, so it was faster than average," he said.[264]

These accounts raise questions about the responsiveness of medical staff to the needs of their juvenile and adult detainees. International standards call for detention facilities to provide children with "immediate access to adequate medical facilities" and provide that "[e]very juvenile who is ill, who complains of illness or who demonstrates symptoms of physical or mental difficulties, should be examined promptly by a medical officer."[265]

A jail's failure to attend to the medical needs of its detainees may subject it to liability under U.S. law. In *Estelle v. Gamble,* a case involving medical care in the Texas prison system, the U.S. Supreme Court held that deliberate indifference to the serious medical needs of prisoners is "unnecessary and wanton infliction of pain" in violation of the Eighth Amendment's prohibition of cruel and unusual punishment.[266] A higher standard of medical care may apply to pretrial detainees, who are entitled under the due process clause of the Fourteenth Amendment to be

---

[263]Human Rights Watch interviews, Montgomery County Detention Center, July 30, 1998.
[264]Human Rights Watch interviews, Prince George's County Correctional Center, July 23, 1998.
[265]U.N. Rules for the Protection of Juveniles, Article 51.
[266]429 U.S. 97, 104 (1976).

free from all punishment; in any event, a pretrial detainee's rights should never be less than those of a convicted prisoner.[267]

Whether or not a jail's medical care is so deficient that it violates the U.S. Constitution, its failure to adhere to international standards and good medical practices carries the risk that serious medical conditions will go untreated, with potentially tragic consequences.

Medical Care for Female Detainees

The jails we visited appeared to make some effort to provide basic medical services with appropriate examination procedures for female detainees, but not all offered regular gynecological examinations. For example, Washington County Detention Center policy provides that if the examining doctor is male, a female nurse must be present during examinations of female detainees. However, the medical staff told us that gynecological examinations are offered only "as needed, if a female makes a specific complaint. They're not offered on a routine basis."[268]

The National Commission on Correctional Health Care notes that

> Research regarding the provision of gynecological services for women in correctional settings has been limited, but it consistently has indicated that such services are inadequate. Annual gynecological exams are not done routinely in either jails or prisons, nor are they regularly performed upon admission. Appropriate initial screening questions about a woman's gynecologic history may not be asked, and in many correctional facilities, there are no physicians who are trained in obstetrics and gynecology, leading to inadequate and inappropriate gynecologic care.[269]

---

[267]*See Ingraham v. Wright,* 430 U.S. 651, 671-72 n.40 (1977); *Martin v. Gentile,* 849 F.2d 863, 870 (4th Cir. 1988) (noting that the due process rights of a pretrial detainee are at least as great as the protections offered to a convicted prisoner under the Eighth Amendment); Michael J. Dale, "Lawsuits and Public Policy: The Role of Litigation in Correcting Conditions in Juvenile Detention Centers," *University of San Francisco Law Review,* vol. 32 (1998), pp. 719-20. The U.S. Court of Appeals for the Fourth Circuit, whose jurisdiction includes Maryland, has applied the "deliberate indifference" standard of *Estelle v. Gamble* to cases brought by pretrial detainees. *See Martin,* 849 F.2d at 871; *Whisenant v. Yuam,* 739 F.2d 160, 164 n.4 (4th Cir. 1984); *Loe v. Armistead,* 582 F.2d 1291, 1294 (4th Cir. 1978).

[268]Human Rights Watch interview, Washington County Detention Center, July 22, 1998.

[269]National Commission on Correctional Health Care, "Position Statement: Women's Health Care in Correctional Settings," in *Standards for Health Services in Jails* (Chicago: NCCHC, 1996), p. 206.

The commission recommends that jails and other confinement facilities provide "comprehensive services for women's unique health problems"; in doing so, "[c]onsidering the unique developmental needs of female adolescents, special attention should be given to their needs" in providing these health services.[270]

While the larger detention centers had separate medical and mental health facilities for female detainees, separate facilities are not always the rule in small jails, raising the concern that female juveniles may be housed with males while receiving medical or mental health treatment. Although we did not see any instances in which female juveniles were commingled with males, in Washington County we observed one adult woman in a cell in the holding area, the only female inmate in a group of cells otherwise occupied by males. She lay on a plastic bed set at floor level, with a single sheet to cover her. The officer accompanying us explained that she had been placed in that cell, plainly visible to the guards and to anybody walking through the holding area, because she was a danger to herself. The officer told us, "It's the best place for her right now because she's right up in front where the officers can see her. We don't like holding females in this area. It's really the lesser of two evils."[271]

Mental Health

While we made no attempt to evaluate the mental health needs of individual juveniles, some children identified mental health services as one of their most significant needs. James S., a seventeen-year-old held in the high security pod of the Montgomery County Detention Center, repeatedly told a Human Rights Watch representative that he wanted treatment to assist him to rehabilitate himself and to help with his mental state. "I just be depressed most of the time," he said. "On lockdown for four months, haven't seen my family since I been here. I overreact

---

[270]Ibid., p. 208. In particular, female detainees report a high incidence of past physical or sexual abuse. According to the Bureau of Justice Statistics, 37 percent of female inmates in jails nationwide said that they had been physically abused, compared to 11 percent of male inmates. Similarly, 37 percent of women and 6 percent of men reported that they had been sexually abused. *See* Bureau of Justice Statistics, *Profile of Jail Inmates 1996* (Washington, D.C.: Bureau of Justice Statistics, April 1998), p. 11. Because of the high levels of sexual and physical victimization within the female detainee population, the National Commission on Correctional Health Care recommends that medical services for women and girls include counseling and other appropriate services to address abuse issues. *See* "Position Statement," p. 208.

[271]Human Rights Watch interview, Washington County Detention Center, July 22, 1998.

to the situation, to the lockdown. I'd like to see if I could get some type of treatment, some help. I want to change."[272]

"There are a lot of mental health needs among the people now coming to the jail. We are not in a position to handle these people at all," Commissioner Flanagan of the Baltimore City Detention Center observed to us.[273] While there has been no systematic study of the mental health needs of children detained in Maryland's adult detention centers, a 1998 study of youth in the state's juvenile justice system estimated that 24 percent are in need of mental health services.[274]

Mental health experts generally concur that youth in the justice system have a higher incidence of mental disorder than the juvenile population as a whole.[275] For example, a 1995 Virginia assessment "revealed that more than three-quarters of all youth in the states's seventeen detention facilities exhibited at least one diagnosable mental disorder. Of that number, 8 to 10 percent had mental health needs in the severe/urgent range and 40 percent were assessed as having needs in the moderate range."[276] Nationwide, the General Accounting Office estimates that between 6 and 14 percent of the incarcerated population, juvenile and adult, may have a major psychiatric disorder.[277]

The Human Rights Watch delegation that toured the Baltimore City Detention Center in May 1999 included a mental health specialist, enabling us to evaluate the mental health services available at that jail. Human Rights Watch researchers were not accompanied by a mental health professional on our visits to the other facilities.

---

[272]Human Rights Watch interview, Montgomery County Detention Center, July 30, 1998.
[273]Human Rights Watch interview with LaMont Flanagan, commissioner, Division of Pretrial Detention and Services, Maryland Department of Public Safety and Correctional Services, Baltimore, Maryland, September 23, 1998.
[274]Deborah Shelton, "Estimates of Emotional Disorder in Detained and Committed Youth in the Maryland Juvenile Justice System," March 1998, pp. 6, 28 (cited with permission of the author); Human Rights Watch telephone interview with Deborah Shelton, assistant professor, University of Maryland School of Nursing, Baltimore, Maryland, June 10, 1999.
[275]*See* John F. Edens and Randy K. Otto, "Prevalence of Mental Disorders Among Youth in the Juvenile Justice System," *Focal Point: A National Bulletin on Family Support and Children's Mental Health,* Spring 1997, p. 7. *See generally* J.J. Cocozza, ed., *Responding to the Mental Health Needs of Juveniles in the Juvenile Justice System* (Seattle, Washington: The National Coalition for the Mentally Ill in the Criminal Justice System, 1992).
[276]Susan Rotenberg, "Responding to the Mental Health Needs of Youth in the Juvenile Justice System," *Focal Point: A National Bulletin on Family Support and Children's Mental Health,* Spring 1997, p. 1.
[277]General Accounting Office, *Mentally Ill Inmates: Better Data Would Help Determine Protection and Advocacy Needs* (Washington, D.C.: GAO, 1991).

Mental Health Services in the Baltimore City Detention Center

Mental health services in the Baltimore County Detention Center are minimal to nonexistent for juvenile and adult detainees alike, with no services designated specifically for juveniles. Baltimore's mental health staff comprises three full-time professional service providers. One of these, a clinical social worker, provides intake assessments for the approximately 87,000 annual admissions at the central booking facility. One masters'-degree-level psychologist works with the women, a population of up to 528 at any given time. A doctorate-level chief psychologist, assigned to work with the men, serves up to 2,428 inmates.

In addition to these staff members, the education program has two part-time mental health workers who provide case management services, but these professionals do not coordinate with either the jail's mental health staff or its corrections staff. The corrections staff includes several social workers, who provide access to the phones for legal and some social calls, coordinate aftercare planning, and otherwise serve as case management staff. The mental health staff with whom we spoke reported that they did not feel that the social workers on the corrections staff worked with them as part of a collaborative team. The failure of staff in all programs to coordinate is a lamentable failure to maximize the effectiveness of available resources.[278]

The paucity of service providers results in the complete absence of mental health programming at the jail—there are no therapeutic groups, no individual counseling, and no aftercare planning efforts.[279] In practice, the only detainees who are able to access mental health services in the detention center are those who are in crisis. Troubling under any circumstances, such limited access to mental health services is alarming when the physical environment of the detention center is taken into account. As described in detail in previous sections of this report, detainees are housed in areas that are largely dark, dreary, run down, poorly ventilated, and infested with roaches and other vermin.[280] Confined in these inhumane conditions,

---

[278]We found a similar lack of coordination between the disciplinary hearing officers and mental health staff. In the absence of a protocol requiring mental health staff to be present during disciplinary hearings, a detainee who engages in self-injurious behavior may be dealt with punitively and without regard for underlying health issues. *See* Part VI, "Disciplinary Hearings."

[279]Article 62 of the Standard Minimum Rules states that "[t]he medical services of the institution shall seek to detect and shall treat any physical or mental illnesses or defects which may hamper a prisoner's rehabilitation. All necessary medical, surgical and psychiatric services shall be provided to that end."

[280]*See* Part IV, "Living Conditions."

detainees—particularly those placed in segregation without appropriate monitoring—are likely to suffer acute exacerbations of preexisting mental health disorders.[281]

The lack of mental health services is especially problematic for juveniles. Youth face greater challenges in adjusting to institutional life, difficulties that are compounded by antagonisms from the street. Because juveniles are a minority population with fewer housing options in the jail, youth at odds with each other may of necessity be housed together, resulting in further need for mental health services. Finally, the lack of mental health services for juveniles is of particular concern because juveniles have longer periods of detention than do adults. Nevertheless, the chief psychologist appeared to minimize the need for mental health services among the juveniles. "They're normally not here based on mental illness," he told us. "Mostly they're very fearful for their own safety on the juvenile section. They feel very safe here. Some get arrested to get back on E Section."[282]

We found that the lack of mental health coverage extends to psychiatric care. On the day of our May 1999 visit, we observed an adult male waiting to be admitted to the Men's Detention Center's inpatient mental health unit. Although jail staff had told us that the facility had psychiatric coverage on Tuesdays, no psychiatrist was on site on the Tuesday we visited. Staff told us that they had not been able to obtain a phone order for medication from the psychiatrist, who was unwilling to prescribe medication for a patient he or she had not seen and was unable or unwilling to visit the jail for a face-to-face consultation. Our observations raise questions about the extent of psychiatric coverage, either on site or on call, that is really available for detainees in Baltimore.

There is no acute care unit for women or juveniles comparable to the men's inpatient mental health unit, which has fourteen beds. The psychologist overseeing

---

[281]"[L]eaving a psychotic or seriously depressed inmate along in a cell to suffer for long periods of time . . . is quite cruel and is likely to cause significant deterioration in their mental condition over time." Declaration of Terry Kupers, M.D., *Coleman v. Wilson,* No. CIV S 90-0520 LKK-JFM (E.D. Cal. Feb. 16, 1993), p. 41. In recognition of the dangers posed by prolonged periods of segregation, the National Commission on Correctional Health Care (NCCHC) requires that all inmates segregated from the general population should be "seen by qualified health personnel a minimum of three times a week to determine the individual's health status." NCCHC, *Standards for Health Services in Jails* (Chicago: NCCHC, 1996), p. 54. NCCHC recommends that juveniles "be checked daily by a health care worker." NCCHC, *Standards for Health Services in Juvenile Detention and Confinement Facilities* (Chicago: NCCHC, 1995), p. 37.

[282]Human Rights Watch interview, Baltimore City Detention Center, September 23, 1998.

services for adult men stated that when juveniles must be placed on suicide watch or provided with other acute care services, "certain statuses are forgiven,"[283] meaning that juveniles are housed alongside adults when they are in need of acute mental health services at the jail.

Detainees with acute mental health conditions are housed in deplorable conditions in a series of dormitories. The patients we saw were naked, with some making an effort to drape their paper blankets over their bodies. Joey N., age seventeen, told us that he was placed in one such dormitory when he was put on suicide watch:

> They took me to the suicide room. That's the butt-naked room. It's a dorm, they got about seven people in it. You don't get no clothes when you're there. I think there was five people including me when I was there. They kept me there for two or three days, then they took me to another dorm where I got my clothes back, then they discharged me and took me back to lockup.[284]

There is no medical justification for this dehumanizing practice, and the fact that juveniles are housed among this group is cause for extreme concern. Moreover, upon inspecting the cells designated for suicide watches, we found that they lacked important safety elements and contained numerous objects and protrusions to which a detainee could anchor a sheet or blanket in order to hang himself.[285]

The absence of a mental health program has likely contributed to the detention center's extensive reliance on lockdowns and similar security directives to address institutional unrest. On the day of our May 1999 visit, children reported that they had been locked down for six weeks, prohibited from taking recreation, making phone calls, receiving visits, or ordering goods from the commissary.

Such harsh security measures are frequently counterproductive, contributing to further disciplinary problems and increasing the need for mental health services. Severe measures that are imposed for a protracted period of time and that punish groups rather than individuals only serve to make the detainee population embittered and recalcitrant.

---

[283]Human Rights Watch interview, Baltimore City Detention Center, May 11, 1999.

[284]Human Rights Watch interview, Baltimore City Detention Center, February 9, 1999.

[285]For example, a suicidal individual would have no difficulty tying one end of a paper blanket to the legs of the cell beds, the other end around his neck, and then leaning backward over the opposite end of the bed.

VIII. EDUCATION

In many cases, the education offered in Maryland's jails is seriously deficient. Although we found considerable variation in the education offered in the jails, several of the county jails we visited offer no classes whatsoever for some or all of their juvenile detainees, meaning that many children are forced to interrupt their schooling for six months or more. Most problematic was the absence of educational opportunities in the Prince George's County Correctional Center. Similarly, we learned that children placed in administrative segregation in the Baltimore and Montgomery County detention centers could not attend school. But even the existence of an educational program was no guarantee that children were receiving the state-mandated minimum number of hours of education. Baltimore instructors and jail staff readily admitted that the jail school shortchanged children almost two hours of classroom time per day, a lamentable practice that they said was necessary in the absence of adequate physical facilities. In Frederick and Washington Counties, as well, our examination of the graduate-equivalency-degree (GED) programs offered to youth raised questions about the extent to which those jails complied with state and federal law.

The failure of Maryland's jails to provide adequate education to juvenile inmates is not only illegal but also remarkably shortsighted. The Center on Crimes, Communities and Culture reports: "In most cases, once juveniles are incarcerated, even for a short time, their line to education is forever broken. Most juvenile offenders aged sixteen and older do not return to school upon release or graduate from high school."[286] For these children, the interruption to their schooling comes at a time when they are statistically most likely to drop out. The practice of offering detained children substandard education—or in some cases no education at all—encourages those juveniles most at risk of delinquency to abandon a critical resource that can assist them to assume socially constructive and productive roles in society.

Education Programs in the Jails Visited

Prince George's County Correctional Center

Asked about the educational facilities for juveniles at Prince George's County Correctional Center, Barry Stanton, the facility's director, replied, "There's no education." He stated that education was his chief priority for the juvenile detainees, noting that he had approached the local school board and the county

[286]The Center on Crimes, Communities and Culture, "Education as Crime Prevention: Providing Education to Prisoners," *Research Brief,* September 1997, p. 4.

executive with his concerns. "The Board is supposed to be providing services for these kids," said Stanton.[287] Teachers at the facility echoed Stanton's concerns. "What kind of education are we giving the male juveniles here? Zero. There's a real frustration on this issue," said one teacher.[288]

The children held in the Prince George's County Correctional Center shared the teacher's feelings of frustration. Brian W., sixteen, said, "I'd rather get schooling in my head than just be sitting here." Jermaine C., who explained that he spent most of his free time playing chess, told us, "I want to go to school. All we do here is sit around and play games." Michael T. remarked, "We don't have no school here. I just read every day, and we play Scrabble. We look up the words in the dictionary and read the definitions. We don't have no one who comes up here and sits down and teaches us."[289]

"In the old jail, juveniles were in the education unit," the teacher told us. "But the ACA requires sight-and-sound separation from adults. That means that I can't put them into my education program until they're sentenced." She pointed out that the strict enforcement of this standard is at odds with the detention center's attitude toward overcrowding. "I'm telling them, 'You'll warehouse the inmates and get a waiver. Why can't I educate?'" Another teacher at the facility agreed: "We were always able to include juveniles until we became ACA accredited about five years ago. Even then, it was just in the last two years that they've told me, 'No juveniles in the unit.' They tell us it's because of liability."[290]

Despite the jail's strict policy precluding boys from attending school with adults, girls at the Prince George's County Correctional Center were in adult classes at the time of our July 1998 visit. The teachers explained to us that strict enforcement of the sight-and-sound rules would inflict special hardship on the girls. "The girls are integrated with the women because I don't care what the rules say. I can't stand to see them locked in protective custody all by themselves," said one teacher.[291]

---

[287]Human Rights Watch interview with Barry L. Stanton, director, Prince George's County Department of Corrections, Upper Marlboro, Maryland, July 23, 1998.

[288]Human Rights Watch interview with a teacher at the P.G. County Correctional Center, July 23, 1998.

[289]Human Rights Watch interviews, P.G. County Correctional Center, July 23, 1998.

[290]Human Rights Watch interviews with teachers at the P.G. County Correctional Center, July 23, 1998.

[291]Human Rights Watch interview with a teacher at the P.G. County Correctional Center, July 23, 1998.

The absence of any educational program for boys detained in Prince George's County is a flagrant violation of state and federal law and international standards. The county must take immediate steps to ensure that all juveniles in the jail have access to an education and that those who qualify for special education are able to receive the services to which they are entitled.

Baltimore City Detention Center

The Baltimore detention center's school, a branch of the Baltimore City public school system, offers virtually the only regularly scheduled activities for youths in the detention center. A critical resource for juveniles held in the city jail, the education program is nevertheless deficient in two basic ways: Boys placed in administrative segregation, one out of every six children held in the jail at any given time, do not go to school; the rest do not spend enough time in the classroom.

The educational program has improved dramatically since early 1998, when there was a minimal education program that was not accredited by the Baltimore Public Schools. At the time of our May 1999 visit to the jail, the school was operating under the same curriculum as the Baltimore City schools and had been accredited by the same authority that accredits the regular public schools. The school offers regular, well-planned programming for youth in general population and protective custody. Notably absent, however, were any educational offerings to children in administrative segregation.

The school is located in four interlocked trailers placed in what was formerly an open area adjoining the jail building. The classrooms are bright and cheerful, with visually stimulating materials on the walls, including displays prepared by the students. The school is a dramatic and welcome respite from the dark and depressing atmosphere in the cells.

Youth admitted to the jail receive educational testing for one or two days and are placed in the school no later than the third day after admission. Juveniles in the general population attend classes between 8:00 a.m. and 11:15 a.m.; those in protective custody go to class from noon to 3:15 p.m. Each class averages between twelve to fourteen students in size, although the school principal told us that there have been as many as twenty in a class. Full with twelve students, the small classrooms would be quite crowded with twenty.

Children we interviewed prior to our September 1998 visit told us that lockdowns sometimes prevented them from attending class. When we asked Commissioner Flanagan in September 1998 whether children missed school during lockdowns, he replied:

> Yes, lockdown disrupts school sometimes. It depends on the purpose of the lockdown. If it's a weapons search, the juveniles go to school. If it's a possible escape, no one moves. If it's some other serious incident, it depends. A serious incident may impede movement. For the most part, the juveniles are the only ones who move during lockdowns.[292]

With the notable exception of boys placed in segregation, who received no education, virtually all children whom we interviewed after September 1998 told us that they attended school even during extended lockdown periods.

The school principal explained to us that because the juveniles' reading levels range from elementary to high school, the teachers explain the substantive materials in terms the students understand. Teachers also employ adult basic education materials that are low in skill level but high in interest. The daily basic classes are English, social studies, math, science, and computers. The school also offers a GED preparation class. The school's computers have learning games and other educational programs that are suitable for individually paced learning, particularly for math and reading. The curriculum is supplemented by enrichment events, including presentations on HIV and AIDS, other sexually transmitted diseases, and substance abuse prevention.

About 30 percent of the youth in the school are identified as educationally disabled. The school has three certified special education teachers on staff, two of whom work in classrooms and the third as a GED instructor. The school operates on the principle of "full inclusion," meaning that special education students are fully integrated into classes with non-disabled youth.[293]

Educationally disabled youth benefit from the fact that the jail school is part of the Baltimore City Public Schools. The city's computerized record system makes it possible quickly to identify youth who have previously attended special education classes; once such youth are identified, the public school system's administrative office faxes the students' individualized education programs to the school. The school sets up meetings with parents to modify each youth's program; according to the principal, the parents appear at approximately 85 percent of the

[292]Human Rights Watch interview with LaMont Flanagan, commissioner, Division of Pretrial Detention and Services, Maryland Department of Public Safety and Correctional Services, Baltimore, Maryland, September 23, 1998.

[293]The school principal emphasized that full inclusion eliminates the stigmatization that special education students often experience. Human Rights Watch interview, Baltimore City Detention Center, May 11, 1999.

meetings. When youth leave the school, the school reviews their programs and sends them back to the students' public schools or to the Department of Corrections.[294]

Teachers may give disruptive youth a disciplinary charge, although the principal told us that teachers do this only as a last resort. In our review of special incident reports involving juveniles, we did not find any incidents in which teachers issued disciplinary charges, confirming the principal's statement that teachers did so only on rare occasions.

The school is a critical resource for juveniles in the detention center, providing the only reliable programming that is available to children. It is rich in resources, with committed teachers and other staff. As a part of the Baltimore school system, the jail school has access to the same books and other materials as the public schools.

Nevertheless, we found two basic problems with the educational program. First, juveniles in administrative segregation receive no education whatsoever, meaning that one out of every six children in the jail do not attend classes. "I think I should be given some type of school program," Joey N. told a Human Rights Watch representative.[295]

Second, those who do attend are not receiving enough time in the classroom. Although the Baltimore City curriculum requires five sixty-minute classes each day, the jail school offers five forty-minute classes per day. The school is accredited on the basis that the school gives youth in the jail twenty minutes of additional instruction per class through homework.

The frank statements of Baltimore City Detention Center officials to Human Rights Watch that they were not meeting the mandated standards, together with the fact that federal law requires that they must certify their compliance in order to remain eligible to receive federal funds, leave little question that as currently operated the school violates state and federal law by not providing the required amount of instruction for general and special education students.[296]

---

[294] An individualized education program is developed for each learning-disabled student once the student has been identified as eligible for special education services. The program must specifically identify the student's educational needs and provide a plan for meeting those needs. *See* 20 U.S.C. § 1401(a)(20); 34 C.F.R. part 300, Appendix C, paras. 36-39.

[295] Human Rights Watch interview, Baltimore City Detention Center, May 11, 1999.

[296] The jail may also be in violation of a consent decree that obligates the Maryland Department of Public Safety and Correctional Services to provide an adequate special education program to all qualified youth in adult correctional facilities. *See* Maryland Correctional Special Education Action Plan, *Melvin C. v. Shilling,* C.A. No. HAR-91-497

The underlying reason for both problems, according to jail staff, is the lack of physical space. "Our biggest problem is space limitations," said Commissioner Flanagan. "The best thing would be to have a permanent building." In order to accommodate the large number of children in the limited space available, the school runs a staggered schedule, and students get only two-thirds of the class time that is required. Commissioner Flanagan emphasized that the lack of physical space also explained the jail's failure to educate the juveniles on administrative segregation. Security concerns, he stated, were not the issue: "We've mixed P.C. [protective custody] with the general population and had no problems. We've mixed the males and the females in school and had no problems."[297]

Whatever solution it ultimately adopts, the Department of Public Safety and Correctional Services should take immediate steps to remedy this serious deficiency in the quantity of education received by all juveniles in detention at the jail.

Montgomery County Detention Center

Montgomery County's detention center offers GED classes taught by teachers from the Montgomery County public schools. At the time of our visit in July 1998, three classes had a total of thirty-three students, with five to six on a wait list. Detainees with high school degrees or GEDs may enroll in community college classes in the detention center, although those who are not residents of Montgomery County must pay for these classes.

Detention center staff and the children we interviewed reported that they attended GED classes approximately three hours each day, for a total of no more than fifteen hours per week. For example, Thomas C. told us that he had attended GED classes every day from 7:45 to 11:30 a.m. William M. reported that he had even fewer hours of classroom instruction, stating that he was in school for no more than two hours each day. As in Baltimore, the low number of classroom

---

(D. Md.); Stipulated Dismissal on Conditions, *Melvin C. v. Shilling,* C.A. No. HAR-91-497 (D. Md.). Even if the school is not in direct violation of the consent decree, which technically applies only to "all correctional facilities and institutions for *sentenced* individuals operated by the Maryland Department of Public Safety and Correctional Services," Action Plan, para. 4 (emphasis added), the jail's deficient education program invites litigation premised on the same legal theories raised in the *Melvin C.* lawsuit.

[297] Human Rights Watch interview with LaMont Flanagan, September 23, 1998.

hours offered to children in Montgomery County do not appear to comply with state law.[298]

Furthermore, the fact that GED classes are restricted to thirty-three students almost certainly means that there are juveniles and some adults who are not receiving the education to which they are entitled—according to detention center staff, there were about forty juveniles in Montgomery County on the day of our visit. We spoke with one juvenile, James S., a seventeen-year-old held in one of the high security pods, who reported that he was not permitted to attend classes. "They say it's because my codefendant is in school, because I can't see or talk to him at all," he said. "I feel I should have the right to go to school."[299]

Despite these concerns, several students stated that they had been able to earn their GEDs while they were in detention. Thomas C. was able to complete his GED in six months and then enrolled in college classes. He was able to complete seventeen credits toward an associate's degree, but he reported that he became ineligible to continue to take classes after he was sentenced.[300]

Other Jails Visited

Both the Washington and Frederick County detention centers offer inmates some GED instruction. In both facilities, the number of classroom hours appeared to fall far short of the state minimum.

Washington County offers one three-and-a-half hour GED class per week. Staff told us that juveniles who request GED instruction are immediately placed in the class. Some children appeared not to be aware that classroom instruction was available. Oliver R., sixteen, reported that he was receiving no education. "Well, I went to an AIDS class," he clarified. "That's the only thing I've had here." Comparing the Washington County Detention Center to Noyse, a juvenile facility he had been in, he said, "You go to school there. You take history and math. I'd go here if they offered it." But Ron P., a seventeen-year-old Washington County inmate, said that he had heard that GED classes were offered at the institution. "I already have my GED," he explained, "so I don't go."[301]

---

[298]In addition, some children expressed concern that receiving a GED rather than a diploma would be stigmatizing for them. For example, Matt P., a sixteen-year-old, told us that he decided not to join the GED program because he hoped to receive his diploma instead. Human Rights Watch interviews, Montgomery County Detention Center, July 30, 1998.

[299]Human Rights Watch interview, Montgomery County Detention Center, July 30, 1998.

[300]Human Rights Watch interview, Montgomery County Detention Center, July 30, 1998.

[301]Human Rights Watch interviews, Washington County Detention Center, July 22, 1998.

We were unable to interview children held in the Frederick County Detention Center. The warden, Rob Green, told us that Frederick County offered GED classes for a total of five hours each week. "Under Maryland law we're required to offer classes. I don't fight with the kids who don't want to go, but we encourage them to attend," he said. Asked about children with learning disabilities, Green replied that the jail is able to get tutors through the Board of Education. He told us that most often the teaching staff are able to identify a learning disability by obtaining the inmate's education history, but "sometimes you just have to stumble upon it."[302]

The Right to Education

The right to education is recognized in both international and domestic U.S. law. Internationally, the right is set forth in the Universal Declaration of Human Rights, the International Covenant on Economic, Social and Cultural Rights, and the Convention on the Rights of the Child.[303] These instruments place an obligation on states to endeavor to make public education available and accessible to all children.[304]

---

[302]Human Rights Watch interview, Rob Green, warden, Frederick County Detention Center, Frederick, Maryland, July 21, 1998.

[303]The United States has signed the International Covenant on Economic, Social and Cultural Rights (ICESCR), *opened for signature* December 19, 1966, 993 U.N.T.S. 3 (entered into force January 3, 1976), but has not ratified it and is only one of two countries that has not ratified the Convention on the Rights of the Child (the other is Somalia, which has no functioning government). As a signatory to the conventions, however, the United States is obligated to refrain from action which would defeat its object and purpose. *See* Vienna Convention on the Law of Treaties, Article 18(a). *See also* Universal Declaration of Human Rights, Article 26.

[304]Article 13 of the ICESCR provides that primary education "shall be available to all" and that secondary education "shall be made generally available and accessible to all by every appropriate means." Article 28 of the Convention on the Rights of the Child recognizes "the right of the child to education," and states party undertake to make secondary education "available and accessible to every child." In addition, the ICCPR, which the United States has ratified, guarantees each child the right to "such measures of protection as are required by his status as a minor," a provision that has been interpreted to include education sufficient to enable each child to develop his or her capacities and enjoy civil and political rights. U.N. Human Rights Committee, General Comment 17, para. 3. On the right to education in international law, see generally Manfred Nowak, "The Right to Education," in Asbjørn Eide and others, *Economic, Social, and Cultural Rights* (1995), pp. 189-211; Roger J.R. Levesque, "Educating America's Youth: Lessons from Children's Human Rights Law," *Journal of Law and Education,* vol. 27 (1998), p. 173.

Although the U.S. Constitution does not guarantee the right to education, all U.S. states recognize a fundamental right to primary and secondary education in state constitutions or confer the right by statute.[305] As the U.S. Supreme Court has observed,

> education is perhaps the most important function of state and local governments. Compulsory school attendance laws and the great expenditures for education both demonstrate our recognition of the importance of education to our democratic society. It is required in the performance of our most basic public responsibilities, even service in the armed forces. It is the very foundation of good citizenship. Today it is a principal instrument in awakening the child to cultural values, in preparing him for later professional training, and in helping him to adjust formally to his environment . . . .[306]

In Maryland, the right to education is guaranteed by the state constitution, which directs that "the General Assembly . . . shall by Law establish throughout the State a thorough and efficient System of Free Public Schools; and shall provide, by taxation, or otherwise, for their maintenance."[307] Admission to the public schools is guaranteed, free of charge, to "[a]ll individuals" five years of age or older and under the age of twenty-one.[308]

In fact, Maryland law provides for mandatory school attendance for most children. All children five or older and under the age of sixteen are required to attend school "regularly during the entire school year."[309] Those who are "habitually truant" from school may be brought before a juvenile court and found

---

[305] *See generally* Molly McUsic, "The Use of Education Clauses in School Finance Reform Litigation," *Harvard Journal on Legislation,* vol. 28 (1991), p. 311.

[306] *Brown v. Board of Education,* 347 U.S. 483, 493 (1954). The U.S. Supreme Court has also observed that education "provides the basic tools by which individuals might lead economically productive lives" and "has a fundamental role in maintaining the fabric of our society." *Plyler v. Doe,* 457 U.S. 202, 221-22 (1982)

[307] Maryland Constitution, Article VIII, § 1. *See also* Md. Code Ann., Education Article, § 1-201 (1998) ("There shall be throughout this State a general system of free public schools according to the provisions of this article."). By law, public schools must be open for 180 days or 1080 hours. Ibid. § 7-103 (1998).

[308] Ibid. § 7-101 (1998).

[309] *See* ibid. §§ 7-301(a)(1), (d)(2) (1998). The mandatory attendance requirement does not apply to a child whose "mental, emotional, or physical condition makes his instruction detrimental to his progress" or whose "presence in school presents a danger of serious physical harm to others." Ibid. § 7-301(d)(2) (1998).

to be a child "in need of supervision."[310] In addition, Maryland law imposes a duty on parents and guardians to see that children attend school; those who do not comply with this obligation may be fined and imprisoned.[311]

The Civil Rights Division of the U.S. Department of Justice has taken action against local jails that fail to comply with state education laws. After investigating the Daviess County Detention Center in Owensboro, Kentucky, the division advised the county fiscal court that "it is clear that the hours juveniles spend receiving instruction falls below that which is required by state law" and that the failure to provide adequate education was among "the conditions and practices at these four facilities [which] violate the constitutional rights of juveniles."[312] The division reached a similar conclusion after completing its investigation in Greenville, South Carolina, finding that children in detention "receive no education and no efforts are made to comply with the Individuals with Disabilities Education Act."[313]

Under Article 26 of the International Covenant on Civil and Political Rights, the United States is obligated to respect the entitlement of every person "without any discrimination to the equal protection of the law."[314] Consistent with this nondiscrimination provision, when a state provides education for its children, it may not arbitrarily deny an education to particular groups of children. The state

---

[310]Md. Code. Ann., Courts and Judicial Proceedings Article, § 3-801(f) (1998). *See also In re Ann M.,* 525 A.2d 1054 (Md. 1987).

[311]Md. Code Ann., Education Article, §§ 7-301(c), (e) (1998). *See also In re Jeannette L. and Shirley P.,* 523 A.2d 1048 (Md. Ct. Spec. App. 1987). The criminal penalties are not limited to parents: the statute provides that *"[a]ny person* who has legal custody or care and control of a child who is 5 years old or older and under 16 who fails to see that the child attends school or receives instruction under this section is guilty of a misdemeanor . . . ." Md. Code Ann., Education Article, § 7-301(e)(2) (1998) (emphasis added).

[312]Letter from Bill Lan Lee, acting assistant attorney general, Civil Rights Division, U.S. Department of Justice, to Buzz Norris, judge-executive, Daviess County Fiscal Court, Owensboro, Kentucky, April 10, 1998, pp. 15, 2.

[313] Letter from Bill Lan Lee, acting assistant attorney general, Civil Rights Division, U.S. Department of Justice, to Gerald Seals, county administrator, Greenville, South Carolina, May 28, 1998, p. 12.

[314]Article 26 further requires that "the law shall prohibit any discrimination and guarantee to all persons equal and effective protection against discrimination *on any ground* such as race, colour, sex, language, religion, political or other opinion, national or social origin, property, birth *or other status"* (emphasis added).

may make distinctions among groups of individuals only to the extent that those distinctions are based on reasonable and objective criteria.[315]

International standards clarify that detention status is not a permissible basis for the denial of education to children. As reaffirmed in the U.N. Rules for the Protection of Juveniles, youth do not lose their right to an education when they are confined. "Every juvenile of compulsory school age" who is deprived of his or her liberty "has the right to education suited to his or her needs and abilities," education which should be "designed to prepare him or her for return to society."[316] The U.N. Standard Minimum Rules for the Administration of Juvenile Justice call upon government officials to ensure that children deprived of their liberty "do not leave the institution at an educational disadvantage."[317]

The children in Maryland's jails are largely pretrial detainees; they have not yet been convicted of a crime. Innocent until proven guilty, they have a particularly compelling interest in continuing their education and ensuring that they do not leave pretrial detention six months to one year behind their peers.[318]

More generally, children in conflict with the law have the right to treatment in a manner consistent with "the desirability of promoting the child's reintegration and the child's assuming a constructive role in society."[319] Implicit in international standards is the view that appropriate education is a critical component of rehabilitation. For this reason, the denial of educational opportunities to children in detention undermines one of the primary purposes of the treatment of juveniles in the justice system.[320]

---

[315]Interpreting Article 26, the Human Rights Committee has concluded:

> It prohibits discrimination in law or in fact in any field regulated and protected by public authorities. . . . Thus, when legislation is adopted by a State party, it must comply with the requirement of article 26 that its content should not be discriminatory. In other words, the application of the principle of non-discrimination contained in article 26 is not limited to those rights which are provided for in the Covenant.

General Comment 18, ¶ 12. *See also* M.J. Bossuyt, *"Travaux Preparatoires" of the International Covenant on Civil and Political Rights,* p. 489 (Martinus Nijhoff, 1987).

[316]U.N. Rules for the Protection of Juveniles, Article 38.

[317]U.N. Standard Minimum Rules for the Administration of Juvenile Justice, Article 26.6.

[318]*See, for example,* U.N. Rules for the Protection of Juveniles, Article 18(b).

[319]Convention on the Rights of the Child, Article 40(1).

[320]The U.N. Guidelines for the Prevention of Juvenile Delinquency note that educational opportunities are critical in safeguarding the personal development of young persons, particularly those who are at risk of delinquency. Article 5(a), G.A. Res. 45/112, annex, 45 U.N. GAOR Supp. (No. 49A), p. 201, U.N. Doc. A/45/49 (1990).

Children with Learning Disabilities

The Office of Juvenile Justice and Delinquency Prevention estimates that as many as 40 percent of youth detained in correctional facilities may have some form of learning disability. Other estimates run as high as 60 percent.[321] Nancy Cowardin, a researcher for the Washington, D.C.-based Sentencing Project, notes that because learning disabilities affect "the learning of social information that is needed for decision making in nonacademic situations," it is "not surprising that learning disabled youth and adults in incarcerated populations represent 3½ to 10 times the percentage found among school children."[322]

The Convention on the Rights of the Child guarantees disabled children effective access to education.[323] The U.N. Rules for the Protection of Juveniles Deprived of their Liberty clarify that children "who are illiterate or have cognative or learning difficulties should have the right to special education."[324] In addition, the U.N. Guidelines for the Prevention of Juvenile Delinquency direct education systems to devote particular attention to programs that provide positive emotional support to young persons and avoid psychological maltreatment.[325]

In the United States, a federal statute known as the Individuals with Disabilities Act (IDEA) requires each state to provide free and appropriate education to children with disabilities if the state receives federal support for educating students with disabilities. Currently all states and the District of

---

[321]*See Alexander S. v. Boykin,* 876 F. Supp. 773, 788 (D.S.C. 1995) (noting that between 17.5 percent and 32.5 percent of juveniles in the custody of the South Carolina Department of Juvenile Justice were in special education programs and that the department's "own investigators admitted that perhaps as many as fifty percent of the juveniles at DJJ are in need of special education"); Robert J. Gemignani, "Juvenile Correctional Education: A Time for Change," *OJJDP Update on Research,* October 1994, p. 2; R.B. Rutherford, C.M. Nelson, and B.I. Wolford, "Special Education in the Most Restrictive Environment: Correctional/Special Education," *Journal of Special Education,* vol. 19 (1985), p. 59; Casey and Keilitz, "Estimating the Prevalence of Learning Disabled and Mentally Retarded Juvenile Offenders: A Meta-Analysis," in Peter Leone, ed., *Understanding Troubled and Troubling Youth* (1990), p. 82.

[322]Nancy Cowardin, "Disorganized Crime: Learning Disability and the Criminal Justice System," *Criminal Justice,* Summer 1998, p. 11.

[323]*See* Convention on the Rights of the Child, Articles 23(3), 28(1)(b). Similarly, Article 26.6 of the U.N. Standard Minimum Rules for the Administration of Juvenile Justice calls upon detention facilities to provide "adequate" academic training.

[324]U.N. Rules for the Protection of Juveniles, Article 38.

[325]U.N. Guidelines for the Protection of Juvenile Delinquency, Article 21(g), G.A. Res. 45/112, annex, 45 U.N. GAOR Supp. (No. 49A), p. 201, U.N. Doc. A/45/49 (1990).

Columbia receive such funding. The act guarantees an education to all children between the ages of five and twenty-one with disabilities.[326] There is no question that detained children with disabilities are covered by the act, which makes specific reference to "children with disabilities who are convicted as adults under State law and incarcerated in adult prisons."[327]

While the act holds significant promise for securing the rights of children who are learning disabled, its principal enforcement mechanism is underutilized. A study drafted under the direction of the American Bar Association's Juvenile Justice Center found:

> While each department of education guarantees that all schools and State-operated programs will provide special education and related services to eligible youth as a condition for the receipt of Federal funds, in reality, the U.S. Department of Education has never withheld any money from States that failed to provide appropriate special education services in juvenile corrections.[328]

The act may be enforced by individual lawsuits, and litigants in more than twenty class action suits have relied on the act to challenge special education services in juvenile institutions.[329] In Maryland, the Department of Public Safety and Correctional Services recently entered into a settlement to resolve a lawsuit brought by sentenced prisoners under the age of twenty-one who qualified for special education services.[330]

---

[326]*See* 20 U.S.C. §§ 1400-1419. Children with mental retardation, deafness, hearing impairment, speech or language impairment, visual impairment, serious emotional disturbance, orthopedic impairment, other health impairment, blindness, specific learning disability, autism, traumatic brain injury, or multiple disabilities are protected by IDEA. *See* ibid. § 1401(a)(1). In addition, educationally disabled children are entitled under IDEA to "related services," such as speech, vision, hearing, and counseling services, that are necessary for them to implement their individual education programs. *See* ibid. § 1401(a)(17); 34 C.F.R. § 300.16.

[327]20 U.S.C. § 1412(a)(11)(C).

[328]Patricia Puritz and Mary Ann Scali, *Beyond the Walls: Improving Conditions of Confinement for Youth in Custody* (Washington, D.C.: OJJDP, 1998), p. 21.

[329]Ibid., pp. 17-19.

[330]Maryland Correctional Special Education Action Plan, *Melvin C. v. Shilling,* C.A. No. HAR-91-497 (D. Md.).

Applicable Correctional Standards

Applicable correctional standards generally fail to protect the right of children in detention to receive an adequate education. Maryland correctional standards—the only standards with which all jails and detention facilities in the state are required to comply—make no provision for inmate education.[331] ACA standards for adult detention centers contain only a generally worded call for "inmate access to educational programs" and fail to address the needs of juvenile detainees.[332] Although a national corrections education group, the Correctional Education Association (CEA), has issued its own educational standards, none of the detention centers we visited employed these standards.[333]

---

[331]*See* Maryland Commission on Correctional Standards, *Standards, Compliance Criteria, and Compliance Explanations for Adult Detention Centers.*(Baltimore, Maryland: Maryland Department of Public Safety and Correctional Services, 1995).

[332]American Correctional Association, *Standards for Adult Local Detention Facilities*, 3d ed. (Latham, Maryland: ACA, 1991), p. 113. This failure to address the needs of juvenile detainees is startling in light of the ACA's express recognition that children may be held in adult local detention facilities. *See* ibid., p. vi. In contrast, ACA standards for juvenile detention facilities—standards that are not applicable to any of the jails or detention centers visited by Human Rights Watch—note:

> The facility should provide juveniles with a broad educational program that is most suited to their needs and abilities and includes but is not limited to: developmental education; remedial education; special education; multi-cultural education; bilingual education, when the profile indicates; and tutorial services as needed. This program should operate under the auspices of the year-round school system.

American Correctional Association, *Standards for Juvenile Detention Facilities,* 3d ed. (Latham, Maryland: ACA, 1991), p. 103.

[333]Released in 1988, these thirty-one standards reflect the first attempt to address institutional and systemwide educational practices in correctional facilities. *See* Correction Education Association, *Standards for Adult and Juvenile Correctional Education Programs* (College Park, Maryland: CEA, 1988). *See generally* S. Adwell and B. Wolford, "Development and Growth of Standards for Correctional Education," *Journal of Correctional Education*, vol. 34 (1983), pp. 123-25.

IX. OTHER ACTIVITIES

In general, the jails visited by Human Rights Watch make an effort to offer regular recreation opportunities to children in detention; nevertheless, children may not be able to exercise enough to meet their developmental needs. In addition, we found that children in disciplinary segregation had almost no opportunities for exercise. In the Baltimore City Detention Center, where children are routinely placed on lengthy periods of cell confinement, juveniles endure a dreary succession of days during which they have little to do but stare at the walls.

We were troubled that the Baltimore jail made only sporadic efforts to provide religious services for juveniles, particularly for Muslim youth. We were especially disturbed to find that jail officials regarded religious services as "privileges"—on a par with the opportunity to order snack food from the commissary and therefore routinely suspended during extended lockdown periods.

Jails offer few other activities for juveniles, sacrificing the opportunity to prepare youth for their eventual return to society. The absence of specialized programming places children held in adult jails at a disadvantage to their peers in the juvenile detention system.

Recreation and Exercise

Although children in most of the facilities visited by Human Rights Watch reported that they have regular recreation periods, the length and frequency of exercise opportunities are often insufficient to meet developmental needs. Some juveniles are given as little as one hour of recreation each week. In addition, those placed in administrative segregation, in high security housing, or on lockup status described days of protracted idleness with no meaningful recreation or exercise and little time outside of their cells. This was particularly true of the Baltimore City Detention Center, where children are frequently placed on extended lockdown.[334]

Dylan C., sixteen, reported in May 1999 that juveniles in Baltimore's general population section had not been allowed to use outdoor yard, the gym, or even the dayroom for six weeks. He told us that during this time, children were allowed out of their cell during weekday school periods and every seventy-two hours for showers. Sam H., age seventeen, stated that during the lockdown periods juveniles

[334]Article 47 of the U.N. Rules for the Protection of Juveniles provides that "[e]very juvenile should have the right to a suitable amount of time for daily free exercise, in the open air whenever weather permits, during which time appropriate recreational and physical training should normally be provided."

spent most of their days listening to headphones, playing chess or cards with their cellmates or with the occupants of adjacent cells, or talking.[335]

The situation is even worse for the two dozen boys in administrative segregation in Baltimore. "No walks, no phone, no visits," Terence B., a seventeen-year-old, told us. "You can't do nothing but sit in your cell. You get that ten-minute shower two times a week. Other than that, stay in your cell all day long. It can drive a person crazy."[336] Asked how he spent his day, Benjie R., age seventeen, replied, "Pushups, sleep, eat."[337] "It ain't too good up here," said Joey N., seventeen, referring to the lack of recreation and the grim surroundings.

> This jail's crazy. I'm ready to cop out, and I ain't twenty years old. It's crazy on lockdown. Ain't got no bars on the doors, it's steel doors on the cells. Inmates locked down all day. They're fucking . . . excuse me, I mean it's ridiculous.[338]

Children held in Baltimore before the extended lockdowns went into effect reported that they had regular recreation periods. Joey N. commented, "The only thing is basketball and weights. You get like thirty minutes or an hour. It's not enough for everybody. Plus they only got like three or four balls."[339] When we visited the jail's gym, in use at the time by a group of adult detainees, we saw two full-length basketball courts, a weights area, a large screen television, and several telephones.The gym was in a poor state of repair, with plaster crumbling off the walls in many spots. We saw some detainees using the weights, but one adult told us that many of the weights were broken. With two full-court games in progress, there was not enough room on the courts to accommodate all detainees. As a result, a large number stood around the court with nothing to do. The gym was extremely loud, almost painfully so, and the ten to fifteen detainees sitting on bleachers in front of the television set appeared to have trouble hearing the movie they were watching.

In Washington County, where children are routinely commingled with adults, we heard that juveniles avoided recreation and exercise out of a desire to steer clear of trouble. "I don't go to the gym," Ron P. told us, even though he is given the opportunity every night. "I think that's a good place for fights. I don't like

---

[335]Human Rights Watch interviews, Baltimore City Detention Center, May 11, 1999.
[336]Human Rights Watch interview, Baltimore City Detention Center, April 30, 1999.
[337]Human Rights Watch interview, Baltimore City Detention Center, May 11, 1999.
[338]Human Rights Watch interview, Baltimore City Detention Center, February 9, 1999.
[339]Ibid.

watching people getting jumped and stuff. That's how people are in here, they'll jump you before they'll fight you one-on-one."[340]

Moreover, we found indications that all facilities, even those with regular recreation periods, may not provide juveniles with age-appropriate opportunities for exercise. Adolescents "require more large-muscle exercise yet are likely to have the same access to exercise as adult inmates."[341] For example, boys in Prince George's County reported that they were usually allowed to use the gym only once each week. "I think it supposed to be two times a week, but most times we only get gym once," explained Jermaine C.. "Sometimes the C.O. forgets, sometimes the gym be full, maybe being used by other units." Asked what changes he would like to see, Anthony P., sixteen, responded that he would like more gym time and games such as table tennis, a request repeated by other boys at the facility.[342]

Girls interviewed by Human Rights Watch gave similar accounts, suggesting that they did not receive fewer recreation opportunities than boys but that, as with the boys, they were not able to exercise enough to meet their needs. Michelle R., held at the Baltimore City Detention Center, told us that girls could play basketball, use exercise equipment, watch movies, or use the time to socialize.[343] Jenile L. reported that girls held at Prince George's County are usually allowed one hour in the gym each week, but the actual time they get for recreation "depends on what

---

[340]Human Rights Watch interview, Washington County Detention Center, July 22, 1998.

[341]Dale Parent and others, *Key Legislative Issues in Criminal Justice: Transferring Serious Juvenile Offenders to Adult Courts* (Washington, D.C.: National Institute of Justice, 1997), p. 5. The National Commission on Correctional Health Care (NCCHC) calls upon jails to provide adult detainees with the opportunity to have exercise involving large-muscle activity a minimum of one hour per day, three times each week. For juveniles, the NCCHC's standard is higher, requiring a daily minimum of one hour of large-muscle activity exercise that is offered on a planned, supervised basis. Exercise that meets this standard includes walking, jogging in place, basketball, table tennis, handball, and calisthenics. *See* National Commission on Correctional Health Care, *Standards for Health Services in Jails* (Chicago: NCCHC, 1996), pp. 58-59; National Commission on Correctional Health Care, *Standards for Health Services in Juvenile Detention and Confinement Facilities* (Chicago: NCCHC, 1995), pp. 49-50.

[342]Human Rights Watch interviews, P.G. County Correctional Center, July 23, 1998.

[343]Human Rights Watch interview, Baltimore City Detention Center, February 10, 1999. The opportunity to socialize is limited by the fact that girls in detention take recreation with the same small number of other girls they see every day in their dormitory. As Commissioner Flanagan noted, "Even when there are seven or eight female juveniles, they have to recreate among themselves." Human Rights Watch interview with LaMont Flanagan, commissioner, Division of Pretrial Detention and Services, Maryland Department of Public Safety and Correctional Services, Baltimore, Maryland, May 11, 1999.

officer you get." She added, "Well, it's supposed to be one time a week, but we don't get to go every week because sometimes there's males in the gym." Diane S., age fifteen, told us that she had not been to the gym in "a while" but stated that the girls were allowed outside after lunch about four days each week.[344]

In contrast, youth in Montgomery County's Youthful Offender Unit reported that they were given frequent opportunities for recreation and exercise, including mandatory calisthenics in the morning. Bruce W. told us,

> There's P.T.—that's exercise—every morning at 4:00 a.m. Everybody's required to do it. If you don't, it depends on the C.O. what they do to you. Certain ones will excuse you. Others will send you to D2 [the segregation section] for about thirty days. That's the same time you'd get if you in a fight. I saw this happen three times.

William M. corroborated this account, stating,

> P.T. is in the morning. That's required. It's okay, it's just the fact of waking up early for exercise. We do jumping jacks, pushups, leg lifts, crunches, stretches, things like that. If you don't do them, you can get locked in or sent out of the program because in this program you're required to do the exercises.

"It's no breaks," he continued. "Just exercises. I don't think it last too long."[345]

Religious Services

In general, the jails visited by Human Rights Watch held regular services for the religions represented in the detainee population. We were troubled, however, by numerous accounts from children in the Baltimore City Detention Center that indicate that the jail does not consistently allow juveniles to attend religious services. According to the accounts of children interviewed between July 1998 and May 1999, the jail has frequently discontinued religious services for juveniles over the past year. Muslim children report that they have few opportunities to attend services for their faith. Finally, we are particularly disturbed that jail staff treat

---

[344]Human Rights Watch interviews, P.G. County Correctional Center, July 23, 1998.
[345]Human Rights Watch interviews, Montgomery County Detention Center, July 30, 1998.

religious services as "privileges" that may be suspended during lockdown periods.[346]

"They had church when I first came here, but I think they just stopped coming. The last time I saw them was around the eighteenth of November," said Paul G., interviewed in February 1999.[347] Dylan C. told Human Rights Watch in May 1999 that the jail had offered Wednesday religious services for a time at the beginning of the year. Corroborating this account, Josh S. stated that services were suspended two weeks before section was locked down; he added that when services were offered, he went every time he was given the opportunity.[348]

As Josh S. did, many of the children with whom we spoke seemed to value the opportunity to attend religious services. "I think it stopped a lot of guys from doing stuff. I thought it was good," commented Shawn G.[349]

Even when services were offered, Muslim youth reported that they were rarely given the opportunity to attend services led by an imam. Evan M. recounted:

> I'm Muslim. Here they have church services every week, but for Muslims it's like once a year. I want to talk to the commissioner about that. The last time they had a Muslim service, I think it was about five months ago. There's guys on the other sections, I don't know their names, they get services every week. We can't go up there to their service because juveniles need to be transported. I would go if I could. I think there's about twenty others on both sides of L Section, too. I don't think it's right. The adults get a service every week, but they stopped letting us go in '97, like at the end of the year. They don't have services for us on the holidays neither.[350]

Finally, when we spoke to Commissioner Flanagan and his staff about the extended periods of cell confinement, the commissioner consistently spoke of

[346]Under Article 48 of the U.N. Rules for the Protection of Juveniles,

> If a detention facility contains a sufficient number of juveniles of a given religion, one or more qualified representatives of that religion should be appointed or approved and allowed to hold regular services and to pay pastoral visits in private to juveniles at their request. Every juvenile should have the right to receive visits from a qualified representative of any religion of his or her choice . . . .

[347]Human Rights Watch interview, Baltimore City Detention Center, February 10, 1999.

[348]Human Rights Watch interviews, Baltimore City Detention Center, May 11, 1999.

[349]Human Rights Watch interview, Baltimore City Detention Center, May 11, 1999.

[350]Human Rights Watch interview, Baltimore City Detention Center, July 17, 1998.

religious services as "privileges" subject to suspension during group lockdowns.[351] Religious services should not be treated as privileges on a par with the opportunity to order snack food from the commissary. Absent some compelling security need to restrict religious services, they should be available to all juveniles.[352]

Extracurricular Programming

Across the United States, "[t]here seems to be no concerted effort to develop innovative programming for remanded juveniles," those who have been charged as adults.[353] With a few notable exceptions, Maryland's jails conform to this national pattern. Apart from limited recreation opportunities and school, children in Maryland's jails generally have few activities to keep them occupied. By failing to offer educational, social, and recreational programs tailored to youth, the state's jails sacrifice a significant opportunity to prepare juveniles for their eventual return to society.

Many of the children interviewed by Human Rights Watch described days of unrelenting boredom, punctuated only by classroom instruction and limited recreation opportunities. "I write raps and sleep, that's it," said Oliver R., a sixteen-year-old in Washington County. Ron P., another Washington County detainee, told us, "We play cards. That's all there is to do."[354]

In Frederick County, Warden Rob Green conceded that there are few programming options for juveniles. "As a pretrial facility, we're limited in the number of programs we can offer. We've got more than most pretrial facilities, though," he said.[355]

Many children appeared to value opportunities for positive contact with adults, opportunities that they were not given in the jail setting. Anthony P., a Prince George's County detainee, stated that he would like to "get someone to come and talk to us and see what kind of person you are. They don't pay no attention. They treat you like dirt. I just wish they'd come and talk to us more.

---

[351]Human Rights Watch interview with LaMont Flanagan, May 11, 1999.

[352]As we note earlier in this report, the extent and length of the lockdowns themselves suggest that the jail routinely and improperly imposes group punishment on detention center inmates. *See* Part VII., "Discipline," "Use of General Lockdowns" section.

[353]Barry Glick, "Kids in Adult Correctional Systems," *Corrections Today,* August 1998, p. 96.

[354]Human Rights Watch interviews, Washington County Detention Center, July 22, 1998.

[355]Human Rights Watch interview with Rob Green, warden, Frederick County Detention Center, Frederick, Maryland, July 21, 1998.

They judge us all the same. They talk about juveniles, but no one comes to talk to us one-on-one like you all."[356]

The absence of positive contact with adults is significant because interpersonal relationships are an important part of adolescent development. As other teenagers do, juveniles in detention look for role models among their peer group and to the adults with whom they come in contact.[357] James S., held with adult detainees in a Montgomery County high-security pod, explained to Human Rights Watch:

> There's lots of things going on, so all I do is keep inside my cell. I sit back and think to myself, because I got problems on my mind. Ain't nobody to talk to. I keep it all balled up inside. Sometimes I want to blow up, but I can't. I don't look to those inside as father figures, but I look to them for what they know. I don't think I should, because they criminals, but what can I do?[358]

Extended periods of inactivity were especially prevalent at the Baltimore City Detention Center. "The majority of the day is programmatic," claimed Commissioner Flanagan when we first visited the Baltimore City Detention Center.[359] Once we were able to conduct a thorough investigation of the facility, we found that in fact most of the children in detention spent their days with nothing to do outside of their limited school hours. Inactivity is even more pronounced during the lengthy lockdown periods that have regularly been imposed since November 1998.

The exception was the Youthful Offender Unit in the Montgomery County Detention Center. Children in the unit told us that they were able to participate in a variety of recreational and educational programming. William M., a detainee in the unit, told us that educational activities designed to help youth address violence and drug and alcohol abuse were offered regularly and that those in the unit had many opportunities to engage in organized recreational activities during their free time.[360]

---

[356]Human Rights Watch interview, P.G. County Correctional Center, July 23, 1998.
[357]*See generally* Robert E. Shepherd, Jr., "Developmental Psychology and the Juvenile Justice Process," *Criminal Justice,* Spring 1999, pp. 42-44.
[358]Human Rights Watch interview, Montgomery County Detention Center, July 30, 1998.
[359]Human Rights Watch interview with LaMont Flanagan, September 23, 1998.
[360]Human Rights Watch interview, Montgomery County Detention Center, July 30, 1998.

X. CONTACTS WITH THE OUTSIDE WORLD

Contact with the wider community—through visits, telephone calls, correspondence, and access to books and other publications—can be crucial to the well-being of detained children. In particular, regular contact with family members and friends can be a significant positive factor in preparing juveniles for their eventual return to society. In general, Maryland's jails provided opportunities for contact with the outside world that met international standards. However, those placed on disciplinary segregation are frequently denied visits, phone calls, and other contacts with the wider community, restrictions which may last for up to ninety days or even longer.

Visits

Each of the jails visited by Human Rights Watch allow most inmates to receive visits at least once each week and generally comply with international standards. Most children reported that their visitors have no problems getting access to the jails. In many facilities, however, children placed on administrative segregation or otherwise disciplined are not allowed to see their family members, a practice which violates international standards.[361]

Such restrictions on visitation were particularly evident in the Baltimore City Detention Center. In Baltimore, children given loss of privileges and placed in administrative segregation are not permitted to receive any visits. The prohibition on visits can last ninety days or even longer. In addition, children in the general population may be denied visits during "lockdown" periods, periods of cell confinement that have lasted as long as six weeks at a stretch.

In addition, we heard from a Montgomery County detainee who told us that he was denied all visits while on lockdown. "I haven't seen my family since I came here," said James S., age seventeen, who had been in the detention center for four-and-a-half months. He described himself as "depressed most of the time" and added, "I overreact to the situation, to being locked down."[362]

We were also concerned to learn that the Frederick County Detention Center restricts visits to twenty minutes each, although it allows detainees to receive visits twice per week. "We have to limit the length of visits because of the number of

---

[361] The U.N. Rules for the Protection of Juveniles calls upon detention facilities to allow juveniles to have visits at least once per week and forbids the denial of contact with family members as punishment or for any other purpose. *See* U.N. Rules for the Protection of Juveniles, Articles 60, 67.

[362] Human Rights Watch interview, Montgomery County Detention Center, July 30, 1998.

people," Rob Green, the detention center's warden, told us. "Actually, twenty-minute visits exceed the standards." He stated that the jail considers exceptions to the twenty-minute limit when family members travel long distances. "If they're traveling in excess of 200 miles, they can request extended visits. We'll consider doubling the visits in that case," he said. He estimated that the jail granted one extended visit per month on average.[363]

A number of children felt that they were not permitted enough time to talk with their family members. Jermaine C., who received half-hour visits while detained in Prince George's County, told us, "Thirty minutes is a problem for my family members and me too. You don't get to talk about nothing. By the time you get to talking, they come in and make you stop."[364]

To their credit, some jails allow visits more frequently than the international standard, which calls for a minimum of one per week. Thomas C., an eighteen-year-old who had spent nineteen months at the Montgomery County Detention Center, reported that he had visits twice per week and could see up to four people at a time.[365] Anthony P. and Jermaine C., detained in Prince George's County, told us that male juveniles were permitted half-hour visits every morning; family members who travel lengthy distances to visit are permitted more time. Diane S. and Jenile L., interviewed separately by different Human Rights Watch representatives, each stated that they were allowed two thirty-minute visits each week.[366]

One innovative feature of the Montgomery County's Youthful Offender Unit is that youth in the unit are permitted contact visits with family members once each month and, in addition, during parent/detainee programs. The children we interviewed appeared to place a high value on the contact visits. "You can actually touch your parents," said Bruce W. "They come in, and a counselor tells them how your progress has been."[367] Nestor S., a Prince George's County detainee who, like all other juveniles in that jail, did not receive contact visits, remarked, "The visits are okay, but I think having the glass between you is a problem. You got these little boxes to talk through. You can only say so much with the glass between you."[368] Similarly, Peter B., a Washington County detainee, told us that he wished

---

[363]Human Rights Watch interview with Rob Green, warden, Frederick County Detention Center, July 21, 1998.

[364]Human Rights Watch interview, P.G. County Correctional Center, July 23, 1998.

[365]Human Rights Watch interview, Montgomery County Detention Center, July 30, 1998.

[366]Human Rights Watch interviews, P.G. County Correctional Center, July 23, 1998.

[367]Human Rights Watch interview, Montgomery County Detention Center, July 30, 1998.

[368]Human Rights Watch interview, P.G. County Correctional Center, July 23, 1998.

that he did not have to visit with his family members through a glass partition. Ron P., another Washington County detainee, added, "It's loud. It's very loud. People yell. You can't hardly hear on them little phones."[369]

Because of the importance of visits by family members and others, Maryland's jails should consider increasing the number and length of visits for children in detention. Jails should also consider permitting juveniles to have contact visits with family members where such visits can be conducted in a supervised setting and as part of an educational or other organized program. In accordance with international standards, jails should never punish children by prohibiting visits with family members.

Telephone Calls

While most children held in the jails' general population told Human Rights Watch researchers that they had few problems making phone calls, those placed on disciplinary status are often denied telephone access for extended periods of time.

In Baltimore, for example, children placed on administrative segregation with "loss of privileges" are routinely denied phone calls their period of confinement, up to ninety days per charge. Indeed, a state hearing officer assigned to the detention center told Human Rights Watch that "loss of privileges," including loss of telephone access, may be extended beyond the ninety-day maximum for segregation.[370]

Baltimore also restricts telephone access when the general population sections are placed on "lockdown," an extended period of cell confinement. At the time of our May 1999 visit, Baltimore's L Section had been locked down for six weeks; the jail denied children access to the telephones for most of the lockdown period, only permitting phone calls several days before our visit.[371] Similarly, Jermaine C. reported that guards in Prince George's County sometimes restricted phone access as punishment.[372]

In addition to denying children the opportunity to maintain ties with family members and friends, restrictions on phone use allow abuses to go unreported and generally foster an atmosphere of distrust among detainees. Several children attributed prohibitions on phone access to a desire on the part of guards to evade scrutiny. Michele R. commented, "When you on lock, C.O.'s don't want you

---

[369]Human Rights Watch interviews, Washington County Detention Center, July 22, 1998.

[370]Human Rights Watch interview with Fred Nastri, hearing officer, Baltimore City Detention Center, May 11, 1999.

[371]Human Rights Watch interview, Baltimore City Detention Center, May 11, 1999.

[372]Human Rights Watch interview, P.G. County Correctional Center, July 23, 1998.

calling home, especially if there be fighting with the C.O.'s or the C.O.'s be banking [hitting] people. It's because of the simple fact of that."[373]

As with visitation, telephone access should not be denied outright as a form of punishment or for any other reason. Even when juveniles are placed on "loss of privileges" or similar disciplinary status, they should have the right to place telephone calls at least twice each week, in conformity with international standards.[374]

Access to the Library

In many of the facilities we visited, we found that children are not routinely given access to jail libraries, in contravention of international standards.[375] "It's hard to get books," said Ron P., held in Washington County. "It's only a certain number of books in the pod. I think there's a library, but I haven't been to it." "Ain't no books unless the inmates have them," Sam H. confirmed. "I usually borrow them from somebody." Asked if the jail had a library, he responded, "I think so. I haven't seen it."[376]

We heard similar complaints from children in Prince George's County. Anthony P.told us that the procedure is that those who want to visit the library fill out a request. Recently, he told us, twelve people put in requests, but jail staff told them that they couldn't accomodate that many people. He reported that he has made three requests to visit the library; each was returned to him. He stated that no one in the juvenile unit has been to the library.[377]

Michelle R., held in Baltimore, told us, "The adults are allowed to go to the library but we're not. We keep asking to go, but they say no reason for us to go. They act like we can't read. When we go to school we allowed to get books. I've heard somebody supposed to come up from the library and ask us do we want anything, but don't nobody ask us nothing."[378]

---

[373]Human Rights Watch interview, Baltimore City Detention Center, February 10, 1999.

[374]*See* U.N. Rules for the Protection of Juveniles, Article 61.

[375]Article 41 of the U.N. Rules for the Protection of Juveniles provides that "[e]very detention facility should provide access to a library that is adequately stocked with both instructional and recreational books and periodicals suitable for the juveniles, who should be encouraged and enabled to make full use of it."

[376]Human Rights Watch interviews, Washington County Detention Center, July 22, 1998.

[377]Human Rights Watch interview, P.G. County Correctional Center, July 23, 1998.

[378]Human Rights Watch interview, Baltimore City Detention Center, February 10, 1999.

XI. CONCLUSION

Maryland's jails are wholly inappropriate places for youth. While some children, particularly those accused of committing violent offenses, may need to be detained pending trial, they do not belong in these facilities. These jails subject youth to the risk of violence at the hands of other juveniles and, in some facilities, from adult detainees. Generally, these institutions, with their imposing physical plants designed to house adults for short periods of time, are simply unprepared to handle juvenile detainees. Our review raised questions about the extent to which staff receive specialized training in adolescent development and behavior management, training which one detention center concluded would make a positive contribution to maintaining discipline and order among youth. Serious deficiencies in the amount of education provided, a dearth of age-appropriate recreational and other programming activities, and concerns that detained youth are not receiving enough to eat to meet their developmental needs contributed to our conclusion that Maryland's adult detention centers are not equipped to address the needs of youth.

This conclusion is particularly compelling with regard to the Baltimore City Detention Center. Youth in Baltimore are housed in abysmal conditions. They face daily risks to their personal safety, at times from fights—"square dances"—condoned and even organized by corrections officers. Disciplinary measures appeared at times to be arbitrary and excessive, with many adolescents receiving the maximum sanction of ninety days of segregation. In addition, jail staff frequently imposed restrictions which were ostensibly justified by security concerns but obviously punitive in nature. Particularly troubling in this regard were the extensive use of "lockdowns," extended periods of cell confinement, usually imposed on entire sections of the jail, and the practice of the detention center commissioner to place some youth on "supermax," essentially a decree that the youth in question would spend their entire period of pretrial detention in administrative segregation.

The most expedient course of action to eliminate these abuses is to put an end to the practice of detaining youth in adult jails. The alternative, undertaking a series of efforts to correct abuses at each of Maryland's twenty-four adult jails, is likely to be time-consuming and expensive, especially in view of the number and scope of the human rights violations documented in this report.

Until the practice of placing children in adult detention facilities is ended, Maryland's county jail administrations and the Maryland Department of Public Safety and Correctional Services must ensure that conditions of confinement for youth in Maryland's jails comply with state and federal law and meet international standards. In particular, jails should offer general education and special education classes that comply with state and federal law and age-appropriate medical and mental health services. For their part, the courts should minimize periods of pretrial detention by expediting cases in which a juvenile defendant is detained. In order to make it possible for the courts to handle such cases expeditiously, the Maryland General Assembly should increase its support for public counsel for those children who cannot afford their own attorneys.

These problems can be solved. With no more than 300 youth in detention at any given time, juveniles in Maryland's jails are a fraction of the total population. By acting in cooperation, state and local agencies can ensure compliance with international standards and secure the safety and well-being of children in detention.

APPENDIX A
Excerpts from the Convention on the Rights of the Child

PREAMBLE

The States Parties to the present Convention,

Considering that, in accordance with the principles proclaimed in the Charter of the United Nations, recognition of the inherent dignity and of the equal and inalienable rights of all members of the human family is the foundation of freedom, justice and peace in the world,

Bearing in mind that the peoples of the United Nations have, in the Charter, reaffirmed their faith in fundamental human rights and in the dignity and worth of the human person, and have determined to promote social progress and better standards of life in larger freedom,

Recognizing that the United Nations has, in the Universal Declaration of Human Rights and in the International Covenants on Human Rights, proclaimed and agreed that everyone is entitled to all the rights and freedoms set forth therein, without distinction of any kind, such as race, colour, sex, language, religion, political or other opinion, national or social origin, property, birth or other status,

Recalling that, in the Universal Declaration of Human Rights, the United Nations has proclaimed that childhood is entitled to special care and assistance,

Convinced that the family, as the fundamental group of society and the natural environment for the growth and well-being of all its members and particularly children, should be afforded the necessary protection and assistance so that it can fully assume its responsibilities within the community,

Recognizing that the child, for the full and harmonious development of his or her personality, should grow up in a family environment, in an atmosphere of happiness, love and understanding,

Considering that the child should be fully prepared to live an individual life in society, and brought up in the spirit of the ideals proclaimed in the Charter of the United Nations, and in particular in the spirit of peace, dignity, tolerance, freedom, equality and solidarity,

Bearing in mind that the need to extend particular care to the child has been stated in the Geneva Declaration of the Rights of the Child of 1924 and in the Declaration of the Rights of the Child adopted by the General Assembly on 20 November 1959 and recognized in the Universal Declaration of Human Rights, in the International Covenant on Civil and Political Rights (in particular in articles 23 and 24), in the International Covenant on

Economic, Social and Cultural Rights (in particular in article 10) and in the statutes and relevant instruments of specialized agencies and international organizations concerned with the welfare of children, '

Bearing in mind that, as indicated in the Declaration of the Rights of the Child, "the child, by reason of his physical and mental immaturity, needs special safeguards and care, including appropriate legal protection, before as well as after birth,"

Recalling the provisions of the Declaration on Social and Legal Principles relating to the Protection and Welfare of Children, with Special Reference to Foster Placement and Adoption Nationally and Internationally; the United Nations Standard Minimum Rules for the Administration of Juvenile Justice (The Beijing Rules) ; and the Declaration on the Protection of Women and Children in Emergency and Armed Conflict,

Recognizing that, in all countries in the world, there are children living in exceptionally difficult conditions, and that such children need special consideration,

Taking due account of the importance of the traditions and cultural values of each people for the protection and harmonious development of the child,

Recognizing the importance of international co-operation for improving the living conditions of children in every country, in particular in the developing countries,

Have agreed as follows:

PART I

Article 1

For the purposes of the present Convention, a child means every human being below the age of eighteen years unless under the law applicable to the child, majority is attained earlier.

Article 3

1. In all actions concerning children, whether undertaken by public or private social welfare institutions, courts of law, administrative authorities or legislative bodies, the best interests of the child shall be a primary consideration.

2. States Parties undertake to ensure the child such protection and care as is necessary for his or her well-being, taking into account the rights and duties of his or her parents, legal guardians, or other individuals legally responsible for him or her, and, to this end, shall take all appropriate legislative and administrative measures.

3. States Parties shall ensure that the institutions, services and facilities responsible for the care or

protection of children shall conform with the standards established by competent authorities, particularly in the areas of safety, health, in the number and suitability of their staff, as well as competent supervision.

Article 4

States Parties shall undertake all appropriate legislative, administrative, and other measures for the implementation of the rights recognized in the present Convention. With regard to economic, social and cultural rights, States Parties shall undertake such measures to the maximum extent of their available resources and, where needed, within the framework of international co-operation.

Article 19

1. States Parties shall take all appropriate legislative, administrative, social and educational measures to protect the child from all forms of physical or mental violence, injury or abuse, neglect or negligent treatment, maltreatment or exploitation, including sexual abuse, while in the care of parent(s), legal guardian(s) or any other person who has the care of the child.

2. Such protective measures should, as appropriate, include effective procedures for the establishment of social programmes to provide necessary support for the child and for those who have the care of the child, as well as for other forms of prevention and for identification, reporting, referral, investigation, treatment and follow-up of instances of child maltreatment described heretofore, and, as appropriate, for judicial involvement.

Article 28

1. States Parties recognize the right of the child to education, and with a view to achieving this right progressively and on the basis of equal opportunity, they shall, in particular:

(a) Make primary education compulsory and available free to all;

(b) Encourage the development of different forms of secondary education, including general and vocational education, make them available and accessible to every child, and take appropriate measures such as the introduction of free education and offering financial assistance in case of need;

(c) Make higher education accessible to all on the basis of capacity by every appropriate means;

(d) Make educational and vocational information and guidance available and accessible to all children;

(e) Take measures to encourage regular attendance at schools and the reduction of drop-out rates.

2. States Parties shall take all appropriate measures to ensure that school discipline is administered in a manner consistent with the child's human dignity and in conformity with the present Convention.

3. States Parties shall promote and encourage international cooperation in matters relating to education, in particular with a view to contributing to the elimination of ignorance and illiteracy throughout the world and facilitating access to scientific and technical knowledge and modern teaching methods. In this regard, particular account shall be taken of the needs of developing countries.

Article 29

1. States Parties agree that the education of the child shall be directed to:

(a) The development of the child's personality, talents and mental and physical abilities to their fullest potential;

(b) The development of respect for human rights and fundamental freedoms, and for the principles enshrined in the Charter of the United Nations;

(c)The development of respect for the child's parents, his or her own cultural identity, language and values, for the national values of the country in which the child is living, the country from which he or she may originate, and for civilizations different from his or her own;

(d) The preparation of the child for responsible life in a free society, in the spirit of understanding, peace, tolerance, equality of sexes, and friendship among all peoples, ethnic, national and religious groups and persons of indigenous origin;

(e) The development of respect for the natural environment.

2. No part of the present article or article 28 shall be construed so as to interfere with the liberty of individuals and bodies to establish and direct educational institutions, subject always to the observance of the principle set forth in paragraph 1 of the present article and to the requirements that the education given in such institutions shall conform to such minimum standards as may be laid down by the State.

Article 37

States Parties shall ensure that:

(a) No child shall be subjected to torture or other cruel, inhuman or degrading treatment or punishment. Neither capital punishment nor life imprisonment without possibility of release shall be imposed for offenses committed by persons below eighteen years of age;

(b) No child shall be deprived of his or her liberty unlawfully or arbitrarily. The arrest, detention or imprisonment of a child shall be in conformity with the law and shall be used only as a measure of last resort and for the shortest appropriate period of time;

(c) Every child deprived of liberty shall be treated with humanity and respect for the inherent dignity of the human person, and in a manner which takes into account the needs of persons of his or her age. In particular, every child deprived of liberty shall be separated from adults unless it is considered in the child's best interest not to do so and shall have the right to maintain contact with his or her family through correspondence and visits, save in exceptional circumstances;

(d) Every child deprived of his or her liberty shall have the right to prompt access to legal and other appropriate assistance, as well as the right to challenge the legality of the deprivation of his or her liberty before a court or other competent, independent and impartial authority, and to a prompt decision on any such action.

Article 40

1. States Parties recognize the right of every child alleged as, accused of, or recognized as having infringed the penal law to be treated in a manner consistent with the promotion of the child's sense of dignity and worth, which reinforces the child's respect for the human rights and fundamental freedoms of others and which takes into account the child's age and the desirability of promoting the child's reintegration and the child's assuming a constructive role in society.

2. To this end, and having regard to the relevant provisions of international instruments, States Parties shall, in particular, ensure that:

(a) No child shall be alleged as, be accused of, or recognized as having infringed the penal law by reason of acts or omissions that were not prohibited by national or international law at the time they were committed;

(b) Every child alleged as or accused of having infringed the penal law has at least the following guarantees:

(i) To be presumed innocent until proven guilty according to law;

(ii) To be informed promptly and directly of the charges against him or her, and, if appropriate, through his or her parents or legal guardians, and to have legal or other appropriate assistance in the preparation and presentation of his or her defense;

(iii) To have the matter determined without delay by a competent, independent and impartial authority or judicial body in a fair hearing according to law, in the presence of legal or other appropriate assistance and, unless it is considered not to be in the best interest of the child, in particular, taking into account his or her age or situation, his or her parents or legal guardians;

(iv) Not to be compelled to give testimony or to confess guilt; to examine or have examined adverse witnesses and to obtain the participation and examination of witnesses on his or her behalf under conditions of equality;

(v) If considered to have infringed the penal law, to have this decision and any measures imposed in consequence thereof reviewed by a higher competent, independent and impartial authority or judicial body according to law;

(vi) To have the free assistance of an interpreter if the child cannot understand or speak the language used;

(vii) To have his or her privacy fully respected at all stages of the proceedings. 3. States Parties shall seek to promote the establishment of laws, procedures, authorities and institutions specifically applicable to children alleged as, accused of, or recognized as having infringed the penal law, and, in particular:

3. States Parties shall seek to promote the establishment of laws, procedures, authorities and institutions specifically applicable to children alleged as, accused of, or recognized as having infringed the penal law, in particular:

(a) The establishment of a minimum age below which children shall be presumed not to have the capacity to infringe the penal law;

(b) Whenever appropriate and desirable, measures for dealing with such children without resorting to judicial proceedings, providing that human rights and legal safeguards are fully respected.

4. A variety of dispositions, such as care, guidance and supervision orders; counseling; probation; foster care; education and vocational training programmes and other alternatives to institutional care shall be available to ensure that children are dealt with in a manner appropriate to their well-being and proportionate both to their circumstances and the offense.

APPENDIX B
U.N. Standard Minimum Rules for the Administration of Juvenile Justice

PART ONE
General Principles
1. Fundamental perspectives

1.1 Member States shall seek, in conformity with their respective general interests, to further the well-being of the juvenile and her or his family.

1.2 Member States shall endeavor to develop conditions that will ensure for the juvenile a meaningful life in the community, which, during that period in life when she or he is most susceptible to deviant behavior, will foster a process of personal development and education that is as free from crime and delinquency as possible.

1.3 Sufficient attention shall be given to positive measures that involve the full mobilization of all possible resources, including the family, volunteers and other community groups, as well as schools and other community institutions, for the purpose of promoting the well-being of the juvenile, with a view to reducing the need for intervention under the law, and of effectively, fairly and humanely dealing with the juvenile in conflict with the law.

1.4 Juvenile justice shall be conceived as an integral part of the national development process of each country, within a comprehensive framework of social justice for all juveniles, thus, at the same time, contributing to the protection of the young and the maintenance of a peaceful order in society.

1.5 These Rules shall be implemented in the context of economic, social and cultural conditions prevailing in each Member State.

1.6 Juvenile justice services shall be systematically developed and coordinated with a view to improving and sustaining the competence of personnel involved in the services, including their methods, approaches and attitudes.

2. Scope of the Rules and definitions used

2.1 The following Standard Minimum Rules shall be applied to juvenile offenders impartially, without distinction of any kind, for example as to race, color, sex, language, religion, political or other opinions, national or social origin, property, birth or other status.

2.2 For purposes of these Rules, the following definitions shall be applied by Member States in a manner which is compatible with their respective legal systems and concepts:

(a) A juvenile is a child or young person who, under the respective legal systems, may be dealt with for an offense in a manner which is different from an adult;

(b) An offense is any behavior (act or omission) that is punishable by law under the respective legal system;

(c) A juvenile offender is a child or young person who is alleged to have committed or who has been found to have committed an offense.

2.3 Efforts shall be made to establish, in each national jurisdiction, a set of laws, rules and provisions specifically applicable to juvenile offenders and institutions and bodies entrusted with the functions of the administration of juvenile justice and designed:

(a) To meet the varying needs of juvenile offenders, while protecting their basic rights;

(b) To meet the needs of society;

(c) To implement the following rules thoroughly and fairly.

3. Extension of the Rules

3.1 The relevant provisions of the Rules shall be applied not only to juvenile offenders but also to juveniles who may be proceeded against for any specific behavior that would not be punishable if committed by an adult.

3.2 Efforts shall be made to extend the principles embodied in the Rules to all juveniles who are dealt with in welfare and care proceedings.

3.3 Efforts shall also be made to extend the principles embodied in the Rules to young adult offenders.

4. Age of criminal responsibility

4.1 In those legal systems recognizing the concept of the age of criminal responsibility for juveniles, the beginning of that age shall not be fixed at too low an age level, bearing in mind the facts of emotional, mental and intellectual maturity.

5. Aims of juvenile justice

5. 1 The juvenile justice system shall emphasize the well-being of the juvenile and shall ensure that any reaction to juvenile offenders shall always be in proportion to the circumstances of both the offenders and the offense.

6. Scope of discretion

6.1 In view of the varying special needs of juveniles as well as the variety of measures available, appropriate scope for discretion shall be allowed at all stages of proceedings and at the different levels of juvenile justice administration, including investigation, prosecution, adjudication and the follow-up of dispositions.

6.2 Efforts shall be made, however, to ensure sufficient accountability at all stages and levels in the exercise of any such discretion.

6.3 Those who exercise discretion shall be specially qualified or trained to exercise it judiciously and in accordance with their functions and mandates.

7. Rights of juveniles

7.1 Basic procedural safeguards such as the presumption of innocence, the right to be notified of the charges, the right to remain silent, the right to counsel, the right to the presence of a parent or guardian, the right to confront and cross-examine witnesses and the right to appeal to a higher authority shall be guaranteed at all stages of proceedings.

8. Protection of privacy

8.1 The juvenile's right to privacy shall be respected at all stages in order to avoid harm being caused to her or him by undue publicity or by the process of labeling.

8.2 In principle, no information that may lead to the identification of a juvenile offender shall be published.

9. Saving clause

9.1 Nothing in these Rules shall be interpreted as precluding the application of the Standard Minimum Rules for the Treatment of Prisoners adopted by the United Nations and other human rights instruments and standards recognized by the international community that relate to the care and protection of the young.

PART TWO

Investigation and Prosecution

10. Initial contact

10.1 Upon the apprehension of a juvenile, her or his parents or guardian shall be immediately notified of such apprehension, and, where such immediate notification is not possible, the parents or guardian shall be notified within the shortest possible time thereafter.

10.2 A judge or other competent official or body shall, without delay, consider the issue of release.

10.3 Contacts between the law enforcement agencies and a juvenile offender shall be managed in such a way as to respect the legal status of the juvenile, promote the well-being of the juvenile and avoid harm to her or him, with due regard to the circumstances of the case.

11. Diversion

11.1 Consideration shall be given, wherever appropriate, to dealing with juvenile offenders without resorting to formal trial by the competent authority, referred to in rule 14.1 below.

11.2 The police, the prosecution or other agencies dealing with juvenile cases shall be empowered to dispose of such cases, at their discretion, without recourse to formal hearings, in accordance with the criteria laid down for that purpose in the respective legal system and also in accordance with the principles contained in these Rules.

11.3 Any diversion involving referral to appropriate community or other services shall require the consent of the juvenile, or her or his parents or guardian, provided that such decision to refer a case shall be subject to review by a competent authority, upon application.

11.4 In order to facilitate the discretionary disposition of juvenile cases, efforts shall be made to provide for community programmes, such as temporary supervision and guidance, restitution, and compensation of victims.

12. Specialization within the police

12.1 In order to best fulfil their functions, police officers who frequently or exclusively deal with juveniles or who are primarily engaged in the prevention of juvenile crime shall be specially instructed and trained. In large cities, special police units should be established for that purpose.

13. Detention pending trial

13.1 Detention pending trial shall be used only as a measure of last resort and for the shortest possible period of time.

13.2 Whenever possible, detention pending trial shall be replaced by alternative measures, such as close supervision, intensive care or placement with a family or in an educational setting or home.

13.3 Juveniles under detention pending trial shall be entitled to all rights and guarantees of the Standard Minimum Rules for the Treatment of Prisoners adopted by the United Nations.

13.4 Juveniles under detention pending trial shall be kept separate from adults and shall be detained in a separate institution or in a separate part of an institution also holding adults.

13.5 While in custody, juveniles shall receive care, protection and all necessary individual assistance-social, educational, vocational, psychological, medical and physical-that they may require in view of their age, sex and personality.

PART THREE
Adjudication and Disposition
14. Competent authority to adjudicate

14.1 Where the case of a juvenile offender has not been diverted (under rule 11), she or he shall be dealt with by the competent authority (court, tribunal, board, council, etc.) according to the principles of a fair and just trial.

14.2 The proceedings shall be conducive to the best interests of the juvenile and shall be conducted in an atmosphere of understanding, which shall allow the juvenile to participate therein and to express herself or himself freely.

15. Legal counsel, parents and guardians

15.1 Throughout the proceedings the juvenile shall have the right to be represented by a legal adviser or to apply for free legal aid where there is provision for such aid in the country.

15.2 The parents or the guardian shall be entitled to participate in the proceedings and may be required by the competent authority to attend them in the interest of the juvenile. They may, however, be denied participation by the competent authority if there are reasons to assume that such exclusion is necessary in the interest of the juvenile.

16. Social inquiry reports

16.1 In all cases except those involving minor offenses, before the competent authority renders a final disposition prior to sentencing, the background and circumstances in which the juvenile is living or the conditions under which the offense has been committed shall be properly investigated so as to facilitate judicious adjudication of the case by the competent authority.

17. Guiding principles in adjudication and disposition

17.1 The disposition of the competent authority shall be guided by the following principles:

(a) The reaction taken shall always be in proportion not only to the circumstances and the gravity of the offense but also to the circumstances and the needs of the juvenile as well as to the needs of the society;

(b) Restrictions on the personal liberty of the juvenile shall be imposed only after careful consideration and shall be limited to the possible minimum;

(c) Deprivation of personal liberty shall not be imposed unless the juvenile is adjudicated of a serious act involving violence against another person or of persistence in committing other serious offenses and unless there is no other appropriate response;

(d) The well-being of the juvenile shall be the guiding factor in the consideration of her or his case.

17.2 Capital punishment shall not be imposed for any crime committed by juveniles.

17.3 Juveniles shall not be subject to corporal punishment.

17.4 The competent authority shall have the power to discontinue the proceedings at any time.

18. Various disposition measures

18.1 A large variety of disposition measures shall be made available to the competent authority, allowing for flexibility so as to avoid institutionalization to the greatest extent possible. Such measures, some of which may be combined, include:

(a) Care, guidance and supervision orders;

(b) Probation;

(c) Community service orders;

(d) Financial penalties, compensation and restitution;

(e) Intermediate treatment and other treatment orders;

(f) Orders to participate in group counseling and similar activities;

(g) Orders concerning foster care, living communities or other educational settings;

(h) Other relevant orders.

18.2 No juvenile shall be removed from parental supervision, whether partly or entire l y, unless the circumstances of her or his case make this necessary.

19. Least possible use of institutionalization

19.1 The placement of a juvenile in an institution shall always be a disposition of last resort and for the minimum necessary period.

20. Avoidance of unnecessary delay

20.1 Each case shall from the outset be handled expeditiously, without any unnecessary delay.

21. Records

21.1 Records of juvenile offenders shall be kept strictly confidential and closed to third parties. Access to such records shall be limited to persons directly concerned with the disposition of the case at hand or other duly authorized persons.

21.2 Records of juvenile offenders shall not be used in adult proceedings in subsequent cases involving the same offender.

22. Need for professionalism and training

22.1 Professional education, in-service training, refresher courses and other appropriate modes of instruction shall be utilized to establish and maintain the necessary professional competence of all personnel dealing with juvenile cases.

22.2 Juvenile justice personnel shall reflect the diversity of juveniles who come into contact with the juvenile justice system. Efforts shall be made to ensure the fair representation of women and minorities in juvenile justice agencies.

PART FOUR

Non-Institutional Treatment

23. Effective implementation of disposition

23.1 Appropriate provisions shall be made for the implementation of orders of the competent authority, as referred to in rule 14.1 above, by that authority itself or by some other authority as circumstances may require.

23.2 Such provisions shall include the power to modify the orders as the competent authority may deem necessary from time to time, provided that such modification shall be determined in accordance with the principles contained in these Rules.

24. Provision of needed assistance

24.1 Efforts shall be made to provide juveniles, at all stages of the proceedings, with necessary assistance such as lodging, education or vocational training, employment or any other assistance, helpful and practical, in order to facilitate the rehabilitative process.

25. Mobilization of volunteers and other community services

25.1 Volunteers, voluntary organizations, local institutions and other community resources shall be called upon to contribute effectively to the rehabilitation of the juvenile in a community setting and, as far as possible, within the family unit.

PART FIVE

Institutional Treatment

26. Objectives of institutional treatment

26.1 The objective of training and treatment of juveniles placed in institutions is to provide care, protection, education and vocational skills, with a view to assisting them to assume socially constructive and productive roles in society.

26.2 Juveniles in institutions shall receive care, protection and all necessary assistance-social, educational, vocational, psychological, medical and physical-that they may require because of their age, sex, and personality and in the interest of their wholesome development .

26.3 Juveniles in institutions shall be kept separate from adults and shall be detained in a separate institution or in a separate part of an institution also holding adults.

26.4 Young female offenders placed in an institution deserve special attention as to their personal needs and problems. They shall by no means receive less care, protection, assistance, treatment and training than young male offenders. Their fair treatment shall be ensured.

26.5 In the interest and well-being of the institutionalized juvenile, the parents or guardians shall have a right of access.

26.6 Inter-ministerial and inter-departmental co-operation shall be fostered for the purpose of providing adequate academic or, as appropriate, vocational training to institutionalized juveniles, with a view to ensuring that they do no leave the institution at an educational disadvantage.

27. Application of the Standard Minimum Rules for the Treatment of Prisoners adopted by the United Nations

27.1 The Standard Minimum Rules for the Treatment of Prisoners and related recommendations shall be applicable as far as relevant to the treatment of juvenile offenders in institutions, including those in detention pending adjudication.

27.2 Efforts shall be made to implement the relevant principles laid down in the Standard Minimum Rules for the Treatment of Prisoners to the largest possible extent so as to meet the varying needs of juveniles specific to their age, sex and personality.

28. Frequent and early recourse to conditional release

28.1 Conditional release from an institution shall be used by the appropriate authority to the greatest possible extent, and shall be granted at the earliest possible time.

28.2 Juveniles released conditionally from an institution shall be assisted and supervised by an appropriate authority and shall receive full support by the community.

29. Semi-institutional arrangements

29.1 Efforts shall be made to provide semi-institutional arrangements, such as half-way houses, educational homes, day-time training centers and other such appropriate arrangements that may assist juveniles in their proper reintegration into society.

PART SIX

Research, Planning, Policy Formulation and Evaluation

30. Research as a basis for planning, policy formulation and evaluation

30.1 Efforts shall be made to organize and promote necessary research as a basis for effective planning and policy formulation.

30.2 Efforts shall be made to review and appraise periodically the trends, problems and causes of juvenile delinquency and crime as well as the varying particular needs of juveniles in custody.

30.3 Efforts shall be made to establish a regular evaluative research mechanism built into the system of juvenile justice administration and to collect and analyze relevant data and information for appropriate assessment and future improvement and reform of the administration.

30.4 The delivery of services in juvenile justice administration shall be systematically planned and implemented as an integral part of national development efforts.

APPENDIX C
U.N. Rules for the Protection of Juveniles Deprived of their Liberty

I. Fundamental perspectives

1. The juvenile justice system should uphold the rights and safety and promote the physical and mental well-being of juveniles. Imprisonment should be used as a last resort.

2. Juveniles should only be deprived of their liberty in accordance with the principles and procedures set forth in these Rules and in the United Nations Standard Minimum Rules for the Administration of Juvenile Justice (The Beijing Rules). Deprivation of the liberty of a juvenile should be a disposition of last resort and for the minimum necessary period and should be limited to exceptional cases. The length of the sanction should be determined by the judicial authority, without precluding the possibility of his or her early release.

3. The Rules are intended to establish minimum standards accepted by the United Nations for the protection of juveniles deprived of their liberty in all forms, consistent with human rights and fundamental freedoms, and with a view to counteracting the detrimental effects of all types of detention and to fostering integration in society.

4. The Rules should be applied impartially, without discrimination of any kind as to race, color, sex, age, language, religion, nationality, political or other opinion, cultural beliefs or practices, property, birth or family status, ethnic or social origin, and disability. The religious and cultural beliefs, practices and moral concepts of the juvenile should be respected.

5. The Rules are designed to serve as convenient standards of reference and to provide encouragement and guidance to professionals involved in the management of the juvenile justice system.

6. The Rules should be made readily available to juvenile justice personnel in their national languages. Juveniles who are not fluent in the language spoken by the personnel of the detention facility should have the right to the services of an interpreter free of charge whenever necessary, in particular during medical examinations and disciplinary proceedings.

7. Where appropriate, States should incorporate the Rules into their legislation or amend it accordingly and provide effective remedies for their breach, including compensation when injuries are inflicted on juveniles. States should also monitor the application of the Rules.

8. The competent authorities should constantly seek to increase

the awareness of the public that the care of detained juveniles and preparation for their return to society is a social service of great importance, and to this end active steps should be taken to foster open contacts between the juveniles and the local community.

9. Nothing in the Rules should be interpreted as precluding the application of the relevant United Nations and human rights instruments and standards, recognized by the international community, that are more conducive to ensuring the rights, care and protection of juveniles, children and all young persons.

10. In the event that the practical application of particular Rules contained in sections II to V, inclusive, presents any conflict with the Rules contained in the present section, compliance with the latter shall be regarded as the predominant requirement.

II. Scope and application of the rules

11. For the purposes of the Rules, the following definitions should apply:

(a) A juvenile is every person under the age of 18. The age limit below which it should not be permitted to deprive a child of his or her liberty should be determined by law;

(b) The deprivation of liberty means any form of detention or imprisonment or the placement of a person in a public or private custodial setting, from which this person is not permitted to leave at will, by order of any judicial, administrative or other public authority.

12. The deprivation of liberty should be effected in conditions and circumstances which ensure respect for the human rights of juveniles. Juveniles detained in facilities should be guaranteed the benefit of meaningful activities and programmes which would serve to promote and sustain their health and self-respect, to foster their sense of responsibility and encourage those attitudes and skills that will assist them in developing their potential as members of society.

13. Juveniles deprived of their liberty shall not for any reason related to their status be denied the civil, economic, political, social or cultural rights to which they are entitled under national or international law, and which are compatible with the deprivation of liberty.

14. The protection of the individual rights of juveniles with special regard to the legality of the execution of the detention measures shall be ensured by the competent authority, while the objectives of

social integration should be secured by regular inspections and other means of control carried out, according to international standards, national laws and regulations, by a duly constituted body authorized to visit the juveniles and not belonging to the detention facility.

15. The Rules apply to all types and forms of detention facilities in which juveniles are deprived of their liberty. Sections I, II, IV and V of the Rules apply to all detention facilities and institutional settings in which juveniles are detained, and section III applies specifically to juveniles under arrest or awaiting trial.

16. The Rules shall be implemented in the context of the economic, social and cultural conditions prevailing in each Member State.

III. Juveniles under arrest or awaiting trial

17. Juveniles who are detained under arrest or awaiting trial ("untried") are presumed innocent and shall be treated as such. Detention before trial shall be avoided to the extent possible and limited to exceptional circumstances. Therefore, all efforts shall be made to apply alternative measures. When preventive detention is nevertheless used, juvenile courts and investigative bodies shall give the highest priority to the most expeditious processing of such cases to ensure the shortest possible duration of detention. Untried detainees should be separated from convicted juveniles.

18. The conditions under which an untried juvenile is detained should be consistent with the rules set out below, with additional specific provisions as are necessary and appropriate, given the requirements of the presumption of innocence, the duration of the detention and the legal status and circumstances of the juvenile. These provisions would include, but not necessarily be restricted to, the following:

(a) Juveniles should have the right of legal counsel and be enabled to apply for free legal aid, where such aid is available, and to communicate regularly with their legal advisers. Privacy and confidentiality shall be ensured for such communications;

(b) Juveniles should be provided, where possible, with opportunities to pursue work, with remuneration, and continue education or training, but should not be required to do so. Work, education or training should not cause the continuation of the detention;

(c) Juveniles should receive and retain materials for their leisure and recreation as are compatible with the interests of the administration of justice.

IV. The management of juvenile facilities

A. Records

19. All reports, including legal records, medical records and records of disciplinary proceedings, and all other documents relating to the form, content and details of treatment, should be placed in a confidential individual file, which should be kept up to date, accessible only to authorized persons and classified in such a way as to be easily understood. Where possible, every juvenile should have the right to contest any fact or opinion contained in his or her file so as to permit rectification of inaccurate, unfounded or unfair statements. In order to exercise this right, there should be procedures that allow an appropriate third party to have access to and to consult the file on request. Upon release, the records of juveniles shall be sealed, and, at an appropriate time, expunged.

20. No juvenile should be received in any detention facility without a valid commitment order of a judicial, administrative or other public authority. The details of this order should be immediately entered in the register. No juvenile should be detained in any facility where there is no such register.

B. Admission, registration, movement and transfer

21. In every place where juveniles are detained, a complete and secure record of the following information should be kept concerning each juvenile received:

(a) Information on the identity of the juvenile;

(b) The fact of and reasons for commitment and the authority therefor;

(c) The day and hour of admission, transfer and release;

(d) Details of the notifications to parents and guardians on every admission, transfer or release of the juvenile in their care at the time of commitment;

(e) Details of known physical and mental health problems, including drug and alcohol abuse.

22. The information on admission, place, transfer and release should be provided without delay to the parents and guardians or closest relative of the juvenile concerned.

23. As soon as possible after reception, full reports and relevant information on the personal situation and circumstances of each juvenile should be drawn up and submitted to the administration.

24. On admission, all juveniles shall be given a copy of the rules governing the detention facility and

a written description of their rights and obligations in a language they can understand, together with the address of the authorities competent to receive complaints, as well as the address of public or private agencies and organizations which provide legal assistance. For those juveniles who are illiterate or who cannot understand the language in the written form, the information should be conveyed in a manner enabling full comprehension.

25. All juveniles should be helped to understand the regulations governing the internal organization of the facility, the goals and methodology of the care provided, the disciplinary requirements and procedures, other authorized methods of seeking information and of making complaints and all such other matters as are necessary to enable them to understand fully their rights and obligations during detention.

26. The transport of juveniles should be carried out at the expense of the administration in conveyances with adequate ventilation and light, in conditions that should in no way subject them to hardship or indignity. Juveniles should not be transferred from one facility to another arbitrarily.

C. Classification and placement

27. As soon as possible after the moment of admission, each juvenile should be interviewed, and a psychological and social report identifying any factors relevant to the specific type and level of care and programme required by the juvenile should be prepared. This report, together with the report prepared by a medical officer who has examined the juvenile upon admission, should be forwarded to the director for purposes of determining the most appropriate placement for the juvenile within the facility and the specific type and level of care and programme required and to be pursued. When special rehabilitative treatment is required, and the length of stay in the facility permits, trained personnel of the facility should prepare a written, individualized treatment plan specifying treatment objectives and time-frame and the means, stages and delays with which the objectives should be approached.

28. The detention of juveniles should only take place under conditions that take full account of their particular needs, status and special requirements according to their age, personality, sex and type of offense, as well as mental and physical health, and which ensure their protection from harmful influences and risk situations. The principal criterion for the separation of different categories of juveniles deprived of their liberty should be the provision of the type of care best

suited to the particular needs of the individuals concerned and the protection of their physical, mental and moral integrity and well-being.

29. In all detention facilities juveniles should be separated from adults, unless they are members of the same family. Under controlled conditions, juveniles may be brought together with carefully selected adults as part of a special programme that has been shown to be beneficial for the juveniles concerned.

30. Open detention facilities for juveniles should be established. Open detention facilities are those with no or minimal security measures. The population in such detention facilities should be as small as possible. The number of juveniles detained in closed facilities should be small enough to enable individualized treatment. Detention facilities for juveniles should be decentralized and of such size as to facilitate access and contact between the juveniles and their families. Small-scale detention facilities should be established and integrated into the social, economic and cultural environment of the community.

D. Physical environment and accommodation

31. Juveniles deprived of their liberty have the right to facilities and services that meet all the requirements of health and human dignity.

32. The design of detention facilities for juveniles and the physical environment should be in keeping with the rehabilitative aim of residential treatment, with due regard to the need of the juvenile for privacy, sensory stimuli, opportunities for association with peers and participation in sports, physical exercise and leisure-time activities. The design and structure of juvenile detention facilities should be such as to minimize the risk of fire and to ensure safe evacuation from the premises. There should be an effective alarm system in case of fire, as well as formal and drilled procedures to ensure the safety of the juveniles. Detention facilities should not be located in areas where there are known health or other hazards or risks.

33. Sleeping accommodation should normally consist of small group dormitories or individual bedrooms, while bearing in mind local standards. During sleeping hours there should be regular, unobtrusive supervision of all sleeping areas, including individual rooms and group dormitories, in order to ensure the protection of each juvenile. Every juvenile should, in accordance with local or national standards, be provided with separate and sufficient bedding, which should be clean when issued, kept in good

order and changed often enough to ensure cleanliness.

34. Sanitary installations should be so located and of a sufficient standard to enable every juvenile to comply, as required, with their physical needs in privacy and in a clean and decent manner.

35. The possession of personal effects is a basic element of the right to privacy and essential to the psychological well-being of the juvenile. The right of every juvenile to possess personal effects and to have adequate storage facilities for them should be fully recognized and respected. Personal effects that the juvenile does not choose to retain or that are confiscated should be placed in safe custody. An inventory thereof should be signed by the juvenile. Steps should be taken to keep them in good condition. All such articles and money should be returned to the juvenile on release, except in so far as he or she has been authorized to spend money or send such property out of the facility. If a juvenile receives or is found in possession of any medicine, the medical officer should decide what use should be made of it.

36. To the extent possible juveniles should have the right to use their own clothing. Detention facilities should ensure that each juvenile has personal clothing suitable for the climate and adequate to ensure good health, and which should in no manner be degrading or humiliating. Juveniles removed from or leaving a facility for any purpose should be allowed to wear their own clothing.

37. Every detention facility shall ensure that every juvenile receives food that is suitably prepared and presented at normal meal times and of a quality and quantity to satisfy the standards of dietetics, hygiene and health and, as far as possible, religious and cultural requirements. Clean drinking water should be available to every juvenile at any time.

E. Education, vocational training and work

38. Every juvenile of compulsory school age has the right to education suited to his or her needs and abilities and designed to prepare him or her for return to society. Such education should be provided outside the detention facility in community schools wherever possible and, in any case, by qualified teachers through programmes integrated with the education system of the country so that, after release, juveniles may continue their education without difficulty. Special attention should be given by the administration of the detention facilities to the education of juveniles of foreign origin or with particular cultural or ethnic needs. Juveniles who are illiterate or have

cognitive or learning difficulties should have the right to special education.

39. Juveniles above compulsory school age who wish to continue their education should be permitted and encouraged to do so, and every effort should be made to provide them with access to appropriate educational programmes.

40. Diplomas or educational certificates awarded to juveniles while in detention should not indicate in any way that the juvenile has been institutionalized.

41. Every detention facility should provide access to a library that is adequately stocked with both instructional and recreational books and periodicals suitable for the juveniles, who should be encouraged and enabled to make full use of it.

42. Every juvenile should have the right to receive vocational training in occupations likely to prepare him or her for future employment.

43. With due regard to proper vocational selection and to the requirements of institutional administration, juveniles should be able to choose the type of work they wish to perform.

44. All protective national and international standards applicable to child labor and young workers should apply to juveniles deprived of their liberty.

45. Wherever possible, juveniles should be provided with the opportunity to perform remunerated labor, if possible within the local community, as a complement to the vocational training provided in order to enhance the possibility of finding suitable employment when they return to their communities. The type of work should be such as to provide appropriate training that will be of benefit to the juveniles following release. The organization and methods of work offered in detention facilities should resemble as closely as possible those of similar work in the community, so as to prepare juveniles for the conditions of normal occupational life.

46. Every juvenile who performs work should have the right to an equitable remuneration. The interests of the juveniles and of their vocational training should not be subordinated to the purpose of making a profit for the detention facility or a third party. Part of the earnings of a juvenile should normally be set aside to constitute a savings fund to be handed over to the juvenile on release. The juvenile should have the right to use the remainder of those earnings to purchase articles for his or her own use or to indemnify the victim injured by his or her offense or to send it to his or her family or other

persons outside the detention facility.

F. Recreation

47. Every juvenile should have the right to a suitable amount of time for daily free exercise, in the open air whenever weather permits, during which time appropriate recreational and physical training should normally be provided. Adequate space, installations and equipment should be provided for these activities. Every juvenile should have additional time for daily leisure activities, part of which should be devoted, if the juvenile so wishes, to arts and crafts skill development. The detention facility should ensure that each juvenile is physically able to participate in the available programmes of physical education. Remedial physical education and therapy should be offered, under medical supervision, to juveniles needing it.

G. Religion

48. Every juvenile should be allowed to satisfy the needs of his or her religious and spiritual life, in particular by attending the services or meetings provided in the detention facility or by conducting his or her own services and having possession of the necessary books or items of religious observance and instruction of his or her denomination. If a detention facility contains a sufficient number of juveniles of a given religion, one or more qualified representatives of that religion should be appointed or approved and allowed to hold regular services and to pay pastoral visits in private to juveniles at their request. Every juvenile should have the right to receive visits from a qualified representative of any religion of his or her choice, as well as the right not to participate in religious services and freely to decline religious education, counseling or indoctrination.

H. Medical care

49. Every juvenile shall receive adequate medical care, both preventive and remedial, including dental, ophthalmological and mental health care, as well as pharmaceutical products and special diets as medically indicated. All such medical care should, where possible, be provided to detained juveniles through the appropriate health facilities and services of the community in which the detention facility is located, in order to prevent stigmatization of the juvenile and promote self-respect and integration into the community.

50. Every juvenile has a right to be examined by a physician immediately upon admission to a detention facility, for the purpose of recording any evidence of prior ill-treatment and identifying any

physical or mental condition requiring medical attention.

51. The medical services provided to juveniles should seek to detect and should treat any physical or mental illness, substance abuse or other condition that may hinder the integration of the juvenile into society. Every detention facility for juveniles should have immediate access to adequate medical facilities and equipment appropriate to the number and requirements of its residents and staff trained in preventive health care and the handling of medical emergencies. Every juvenile who is ill, who complains of illness or who demonstrates symptoms of physical or mental difficulties, should be examined promptly by a medical officer.

52. Any medical officer who has reason to believe that the physical or mental health of a juvenile has been or will be injuriously affected by continued detention, a hunger strike or any condition of detention should report this fact immediately to the director of the detention facility in question and to the independent authority responsible for safeguarding the well-being of the juvenile.

53. A juvenile who is suffering from mental illness should be treated in a specialized institution under independent medical management. Steps should be taken, by arrangement with appropriate agencies, to ensure any necessary continuation of mental health care after release.

54. Juvenile detention facilities should adopt specialized drug abuse prevention and rehabilitation programmes administered by qualified personnel. These programmes should be adapted to the age, sex and other requirements of the juveniles concerned, and detoxification facilities and services staffed by trained personnel should be available to drug- or alcohol-dependent juveniles.

55. Medicines should be administered only for necessary treatment on medical grounds and, when possible, after having obtained the informed consent of the juvenile concerned. In particular, they must not be administered with a view to eliciting information or a confession, as a punishment or as a means of restraint. Juveniles shall never be testers in the experimental use of drugs and treatment. The administration of any drug should always be authorized and carried out by qualified medical personnel.

I. Notification of illness, injury and death

56. The family or guardian of a juvenile and any other person designated by the juvenile have the right to be informed of the state of health of the juvenile on request and

in the event of any important changes in the health of the juvenile. The director of the detention facility should notify immediately the family or guardian of the juvenile concerned, or other designated person, in case of death, illness requiring transfer of the juvenile to an outside medical facility, or a condition requiring clinical care within the detention facility for more than 48 hours. Notification should also be given to the consular authorities of the State of which a foreign juvenile is a citizen.

57. Upon the death of a juvenile during the period of deprivation of liberty, the nearest relative should have the right to inspect the death certificate, see the body and determine the method of disposal of the body. Upon the death of a juvenile in detention, there should be an independent inquiry into the causes of death, the report of which should be made accessible to the nearest relative. This inquiry should also be made when the death of a juvenile occurs within six months from the date of his or her release from the detention facility and there is reason to believe that the death is related to the period of detention.

58. A juvenile should be informed at the earliest possible time of the death, serious illness or injury of any immediate family member and should be provided with the opportunity to attend the funeral of the deceased or go to the bedside of a critically ill relative.

J. Contacts with the wider community

59. Every means should be provided to ensure that juveniles have adequate communication with the outside world, which is an integral part of the right to fair and humane treatment and is essential to the preparation of juveniles for their return to society. Juveniles should be allowed to communicate with their families, friends and other persons or representatives of reputable outside organizations, to leave detention facilities for a visit to their home and family and to receive special permission to leave the detention facility for educational, vocational or other important reasons. Should the juvenile be serving a sentence, the time spent outside a detention facility should be counted as part of the period of sentence.

60. Every juvenile should have the right to receive regular and frequent visits, in principle once a week and not less than once a month, in circumstances that respect the need of the juvenile for privacy, contact and unrestricted communication with the family and the defense counsel.

61. Every juvenile should have the right to communicate in writing or by telephone at least twice a week

with the person of his or her choice, unless legally restricted, and should be assisted as necessary in order effectively to enjoy this right. Every juvenile should have the right to receive correspondence.

62. Juveniles should have the opportunity to keep themselves informed regularly of the news by reading newspapers, periodicals and other publications, through access to radio and television programmes and motion pictures, and through the visits of the representatives of any lawful club or organization in which the juvenile is interested.

K. Limitations of physical restraint and the use of force

63. Recourse to instruments of restraint and to force for any purpose should be prohibited, except as set forth in rule 64 below.

64. Instruments of restraint and force can only be used in exceptional cases, where all other control methods have been exhausted and failed, and only as explicitly authorized and specified by law and regulation. They should not cause humiliation or degradation, and should be used restrictively and only for the shortest possible period of time. By order of the director of the administration, such instruments might be resorted to in order to prevent the juvenile from inflicting self-injury, injuries to others or serious destruction of property. In such instances, the director should at once consult medical and other relevant personnel and report to the higher administrative authority.

65. The carrying and use of weapons by personnel should be prohibited in any facility where juveniles are detained.

L. Disciplinary procedures

66. Any disciplinary measures and procedures should maintain the interest of safety and an ordered community life and should be consistent with the upholding of the inherent dignity of the juvenile and the fundamental objective of institutional care, namely, instilling a sense of justice, self-respect and respect for the basic rights of every person.

67. All disciplinary measures constituting cruel, inhuman or degrading treatment shall be strictly prohibited, including corporal punishment, placement in a dark cell, closed or solitary confinement or any other punishment that may compromise the physical or mental health of the juvenile concerned. The reduction of diet and the restriction or denial of contact with family members should be prohibited for any purpose. Labor should always be viewed as an educational tool and a means of promoting the self-respect of the juvenile in preparing him or her for return to the community and

should not be imposed as a disciplinary sanction. No juvenile should be sanctioned more than once for the same disciplinary infraction. Collective sanctions should be prohibited.

68. Legislation or regulations adopted by the competent administrative authority should establish norms concerning the following, taking full account of the fundamental characteristics, needs and rights of juveniles:

(a) Conduct constituting a disciplinary offense;

(b) Type and duration of disciplinary sanctions that may be inflicted;

(c) The authority competent to impose such sanctions;

(d) The authority competent to consider appeals.

69. A report of misconduct should be presented promptly to the competent authority, which should decide on it without undue delay. The competent authority should conduct a thorough examination of the case.

70. No juvenile should be disciplinarily sanctioned except in strict accordance with the terms of the law and regulations in force. No juvenile should be sanctioned unless he or she has been informed of the alleged infraction in a manner appropriate to the full understanding of the juvenile, and given a proper opportunity of presenting his or her defense, including the right of appeal to a competent impartial authority. Complete records should be kept of all disciplinary proceedings.

71. No juveniles should be responsible for disciplinary functions except in the supervision of specified social, educational or sports activities or in self-government programmes.

M. Inspection and complaints

72. Qualified inspectors or an equivalent duly constituted authority not belonging to the administration of the facility should be empowered to conduct inspections on a regular basis and to undertake unannounced inspections on their own initiative, and should enjoy full guarantees of independence in the exercise of this function. Inspectors should have unrestricted access to all persons employed by or working in any facility where juveniles are or may be deprived of their liberty, to all juveniles and to all records of such facilities.

73. Qualified medical officers attached to the inspecting authority or the public health service should participate in the inspections, evaluating compliance with the rules concerning the physical environment, hygiene, accommodation, food, exercise and medical services, as well as any other aspect or conditions of institutional life that affect the

physical and mental health of juveniles. Every juvenile should have the right to talk in confidence to any inspecting officer.

74. After completing the inspection, the inspector should be required to submit a report on the findings. The report should include an evaluation of the compliance of the detention facilities with the present rules and relevant provisions of national law, and recommendations regarding any steps considered necessary to ensure compliance with them. Any facts discovered by an inspector that appear to indicate that a violation of legal provisions concerning the rights of juveniles or the operation of a juvenile detention facility has occurred should be communicated to the competent authorities for investigation and prosecution.

75. Every juvenile should have the opportunity of making requests or complaints to the director of the detention facility and to his or her authorized representative.

76. Every juvenile should have the right to make a request or complaint, without censorship as to substance, to the central administration, the judicial authority or other proper authorities through approved channels, and to be informed of the response without delay.

77. Efforts should be made to establish an independent office (ombudsman) to receive and investigate complaints made by juveniles deprived of their liberty and to assist in the achievement of equitable settlements.

78. Every juvenile should have the right to request assistance from family members, legal counselors, humanitarian groups or others where possible, in order to make a complaint. Illiterate juveniles should be provided with assistance should they need to use the services of public or private agencies and organizations which provide legal counsel or which are competent to receive complaints.

N. Return to the community

79. All juveniles should benefit from arrangements designed to assist them in returning to society, family life, education or employment after release. Procedures, including early release, and special courses should be devised to this end.

80. Competent authorities should provide or ensure services to assist juveniles in re-establishing themselves in society and to lessen prejudice against such juveniles. These services should ensure', to the extent possible, that the juvenile is provided with suitable residence, employment, clothing, and sufficient means to maintain himself or herself upon release in order to facilitate successful reintegration. The

representatives of agencies providing such services should be consulted and should have access to juveniles while detained, with a view to assisting them in their return to the community.

V. Personnel

81. Personnel should be qualified and include a sufficient number of specialists such as educators, vocational instructors, counselors, social workers, psychiatrists and psychologists. These and other specialist staff should normally be employed on a permanent basis. This should not preclude part-time or volunteer workers when the level of support and training they can provide is appropriate and beneficial. Detention facilities should make use of all remedial, educational, moral, spiritual, and other resources and forms of assistance that are appropriate and available in the community, according to the individual needs and problems of detained juveniles.

82. The administration should provide for the careful selection and recruitment of every grade and type of personnel, since the proper management of detention facilities depends on their integrity, humanity, ability and professional capacity to deal with juveniles, as well as personal suitability for the work.

83. To secure the foregoing ends, personnel should be appointed as professional officers with adequate remuneration to attract and retain suitable women and men. The personnel of juvenile detention facilities should be continually encouraged to fulfil their duties and obligations in a humane, committed, professional, fair and efficient manner, to conduct themselves at all times in such a way as to deserve and gain the respect of the juveniles, and to provide juveniles with a positive role model and perspective.

84. The administration should introduce forms of organization and management that facilitate communications between different categories of staff in each detention facility so as to enhance cooperation between the various services engaged in the care of juveniles, as well as between staff and the administration, with a view to ensuring that staff directly in contact with juveniles are able to function in conditions favorable to the efficient fulfilment of their duties.

85. The personnel should receive such training as will enable them to carry out their responsibilities effectively, in particular training in child psychology, child welfare and international standards and norms of human rights and the rights of the child, including the present Rules. The personnel should maintain and

improve their knowledge and professional capacity by attending courses of in-service training, to be organized at suitable intervals throughout their career.

86. The director of a facility should be adequately qualified for his or her task, with administrative ability and suitable training and experience, and should carry out his or her duties on a full-time basis.

87. In the performance of their duties, personnel of detention facilities should respect and protect the human dignity and fundamental human rights of all juveniles, in particular, as follows:

(a) No member of the detention facility or institutional personnel may inflict, instigate or tolerate any act of torture or any form of harsh, cruel, inhuman or degrading treatment, punishment, correction or discipline under any pretext or circumstance whatsoever;

(b) All personnel should rigorously oppose and combat any act of corruption, reporting it without delay to the competent authorities;

(c) All personnel should respect the present Rules. Personnel who have reason to believe that a serious violation of the present Rules has occurred or is about to occur should report the matter to their superior authorities or organs vested with reviewing or remedial power;

(d) All personnel should ensure the full protection of the physical and mental health of juveniles, including protection from physical, sexual and emotional abuse and exploitation, and should take immediate action to secure medical attention whenever required;

(e) All personnel should respect the right of the juvenile to privacy, and, in particular, should safeguard all confidential matters concerning juveniles or their families learned as a result of their professional capacity;

(f) All personnel should seek to minimize any differences between life inside and outside the detention facility which tend to lessen due respect for the dignity of juveniles as human beings.

Appendix D
Standard Minimum Rules for the Treatment of Prisoners

Preliminary Observations

1. The following rules are not intended to describe in detail a model system of penal institutions. They seek only, on the basis of the general consensus of contemporary thought and the essential elements of the most adequate systems of today, to set out what is generally accepted as being good principle and practice in the treatment of prisoners and the management of institutions.

2. In view of the great variety of legal, social, economic and geographical conditions of the world, it is evident that not all of the rules are capable of application in all places and at all times. They should, however, serve to stimulate a constant endeavor to overcome practical difficulties in the way of their application, in the knowledge that they represent, as a whole, the minimum conditions which are accepted as suitable by the United Nations.

3. On the other hand, the rules cover a field in which thought is constantly developing. They are not intended to preclude experiment and practices, provided these are in harmony with the principles and seek to further the purposes which derive from the text of the rules as a whole. It will always be justifiable for the central prison administration to authorize departures from the rules in this spirit.

4. (1) Part I of the rules covers the general management of institutions, and is applicable to all categories of prisoners, criminal or civil, untried or convicted, including prisoners subject to "security measures" or corrective measures ordered by the judge.

(2) Part II contains rules applicable only to the special categories dealt with in each section. Nevertheless, the rules under section A, applicable to prisoners under sentence, shall be equally applicable to categories of prisoners dealt with in sections B, C and D, provided they do not conflict with the rules governing those categories and are for their benefit.

5. (1) The rules do not seek to regulate the management of institutions set aside for young persons such as Borstal institutions or correctional schools, but in general part I would be equally applicable in such institutions.

(2) The category of young prisoners should include at least all young persons who come within the jurisdiction of juvenile courts. As a rule, such young persons should not be sentenced to imprisonment.

PART I: RULES OF GENERAL APPLICATION

Basic principle

6. (1) The following rules shall be applied impartially. There shall be no discrimination on grounds of race, color, sex, language, religion, political or other opinion, national or social origin, property, birth or other status.

(2) On the other hand, it is necessary to respect the religious beliefs and moral precepts of the group to which a prisoner belongs.

Register

7. (1) In every place where persons are imprisoned there shall be kept a bound registration book with numbered pages in which shall be entered in respect of each prisoner received:

(a) Information concerning his identity;

(b) The reasons for his commitment and the authority therefor;

(c) The day and hour of his admission and release.

(2) No person shall be received in an institution without a valid commitment order of which the details shall have been previously entered in the register. Separation of categories

8. The different categories of prisoners shall be kept in separate institutions or parts of institutions taking account of their sex, age, criminal record, the legal reason for their detention and the necessities of their treatment. Thus,

(a) Men and women shall so far as possible be detained in separate institutions; in an institution which receives both men and women the whole of the premises allocated to women shall be entirely separate;

(b) Untried prisoners shall be kept separate from convicted prisoners;

(c) Persons imprisoned for debt and other civil prisoners shall be kept separate from persons imprisoned by reason of a criminal offense;

(d) Young prisoners shall be kept separate from adults.

Accommodation

9. (1) Where sleeping accommodation is in individual cells or rooms, each prisoner shall occupy by night a cell or room by himself. If for special reasons, such as temporary overcrowding, it becomes necessary for the central prison administration to make an exception to this rule, it is not desirable to have two prisoners in a cell or room.

(2) Where dormitories are used, they shall be occupied by prisoners carefully selected as being suitable to associate with one another in

those conditions. There shall be regular supervision by night, in keeping with the nature of the institution.

10. All accommodation provided for the use of prisoners and in particular all sleeping accommodation shall meet all requirements of health, due regard being paid to climatic conditions and particularly to cubic content of air, minimum floor space, lighting, heating and ventilation.

11. In all places where prisoners are required to live or work,

(a) The windows shall be large enough to enable the prisoners to read or work by natural light, and shall be so constructed that they can allow the entrance of fresh air whether or not there is artificial ventilation;

(b) Artificial light shall be provided sufficient for the prisoners to read or work without injury to eyesight.

12. The sanitary installations shall be adequate to enable every prisoner to comply with the needs of nature when necessary and in a clean and decent manner.

13. Adequate bathing and shower installations shall be provided so that every prisoner may be enabled and required to have a bath or shower, at a temperature suitable to the climate, as frequently as necessary for general hygiene according to season and geographical region, but at least once a week in a temperate climate.

14. All pans of an institution regularly used by prisoners shall be properly maintained and kept scrupulously clean at all times.

Personal hygiene

15. Prisoners shall be required to keep their persons clean, and to this end they shall be provided with water and with such toilet articles as are necessary for health and cleanliness.

16. In order that prisoners may maintain a good appearance compatible with their self-respect, facilities shall be provided for the proper care of the hair and beard, and men shall be enabled to shave regularly.

Clothing and bedding

17. (1) Every prisoner who is not allowed to wear his own clothing shall be provided with an outfit of clothing suitable for the climate and adequate to keep him in good health. Such clothing shall in no manner be degrading or humiliating.

(2) All clothing shall be clean and kept in proper condition. Underclothing shall be changed and washed as often as necessary for the maintenance of hygiene.

(3) In exceptional circumstances, whenever a prisoner

is removed outside the institution for an authorized purpose, he shall be allowed to wear his own clothing or other inconspicuous clothing.

18. If prisoners are allowed to wear their own clothing, arrangements shall be made on their admission to the institution to ensure that it shall be clean and fit for use.

19. Every prisoner shall, in accordance with local or national standards, be provided with a separate bed, and with separate and sufficient bedding which shall be clean when issued, kept in good order and changed often enough to ensure its cleanliness.

Food

20. (1) Every prisoner shall be provided by the administration at the usual hours with food of nutritional value adequate for health and strength, of wholesome quality and well prepared and served.

(2) Drinking water shall be available to every prisoner whenever he needs it.

Exercise and sport

21. (1) Every prisoner who is not employed in outdoor work shall have at least one hour of suitable exercise in the open air daily if the weather permits.

(2) Young prisoners, and others of suitable age and physique, shall receive physical and recreational training during the period of exercise. To this end space, installations and equipment should be provided.

Medical services

22. (1) At every institution there shall be available the services of at least one qualified medical officer who should have some knowledge of psychiatry. The medical services should be organized in close relationship to the general health administration of the community or nation. They shall include a psychiatric service for the diagnosis and, in proper cases, the treatment of states of mental abnormality.

(2) Sick prisoners who require specialist treatment shall be transferred to specialized institutions or to civil hospitals. Where hospital facilities are provided in an institution, their equipment, furnishings and pharmaceutical supplies shall be proper for the medical care and treatment of sick prisoners, and there shall be a staff of suitable trained officers.

(3) The services of a qualified dental officer shall be available to every prisoner.

23. (1) In women's institutions there shall be special accommodation for all necessary pre-natal and post-natal care and treatment. Arrangements shall be

made wherever practicable for children to be torn in a hospital outside the institution. If a child is born in prison, this fact shall not be mentioned in the birth certificate.

(2) Where nursing infants are allowed to remain in the institution with their mothers, provision shall be made for a nursery staffed by qualified persons, where the infants shall be placed when they are not in the care of their mothers.

24. The medical officer shall see and examine every prisoner as soon as possible after his admission and thereafter as necessary, with a view particularly to the discovery of physical or mental illness and the taking of all necessary measures; the segregation of prisoners suspected of infectious or contagious conditions; the noting of physical or mental defects which might hamper rehabilitation, and the determination of the physical capacity of every prisoner for work.

25. (1) The medical officer shall have the care of the physical and mental health of the prisoners and should daily see all sick prisoners, all who complain of illness, and any prisoner to whom his attention is specially directed.

(2) The medical officer shall report to the director whenever he considers that a prisoner's physical or mental health has been or will be injuriously affected by continued imprisonment or by any condition of imprisonment.

26. (1) The medical officer shall regularly inspect and advise the director upon:

(a) The quantity, quality, preparation and service of food;

(b) The hygiene and cleanliness of the institution and the prisoners;

(c) The sanitation, heating, lighting and ventilation of the institution;

(d) The suitability and cleanliness of the prisoners' clothing and bedding;

(e) The observance of the rules concerning physical education and sports, in cases where there is no technical personnel in charge of these activities.

(2) The director shall take into consideration the reports and advice that the medical officer submits according to rules 25 (2) and 26 and, in case he concurs with the recommendations made, shall take immediate steps to give effect to those recommendations; if they are not within his competence or if he does not concur with them, he shall immediately submit his own report and the advice of the medical officer to higher authority.

Discipline and punishment

27. Discipline and order shall be maintained with firmness, but

with no more restriction than is necessary for safe custody and well-ordered community life.

28. (1) No prisoner shall be employed, in the service of the institution, in any disciplinary capacity.

(2) This rule shall not, however, impede the proper functioning of systems based on self-government, under which specified social, educational or sports activities or responsibilities are entrusted, under supervision, to prisoners who are formed into groups for the purposes of treatment.

29. The following shall always be determined by the law or by the regulation of the competent administrative authority:

(a) Conduct constituting a disciplinary offense;

(b) The types and duration of punishment which may be inflicted;

(c) The authority competent to impose such punishment.

30. (1) No prisoner shall be punished except in accordance with the terms of such law or regulation, and never twice for the same offense.

(2) No prisoner shall be punished unless he has been informed of the offense alleged against him and given a proper opportunity of presenting his defense. The competent authority shall conduct a thorough examination of the case.

(3) Where necessary and practicable the prisoner shall be allowed to make his defense through an interpreter.

31. Corporal punishment, punishment by placing in a dark cell, and all cruel, inhuman or degrading punishments shall be completely prohibited as punishments for disciplinary offenses.

32. (1) Punishment by close confinement or reduction of diet shall never be inflicted unless the medical officer has examined the prisoner and certified in writing that he is fit to sustain it.

(2) The same shall apply to any other punishment that may be prejudicial to the physical or mental health of a prisoner. In no case may such punishment be contrary to or depart from the principle stated in rule 31.

(3) The medical officer shall visit daily prisoners undergoing such punishments and shall advise the director if he considers the termination or alteration of the punishment necessary on grounds of physical or mental health.

Instruments of restraint

33. Instruments of restraint, such as handcuffs, chains, irons and strait-jacket, shall never be applied as a punishment. Furthermore, chains or irons shall not be used as

restraints. Other instruments of restraint shall not be used except in the following circumstances:

(a) As a precaution against escape during a transfer, provided that they shall be removed when the prisoner appears before a judicial or administrative authority;

(b) On medical grounds by direction of the medical officer;

(c) By order of the director, if other methods of control fail, in order to prevent a prisoner from injuring himself or others or from damaging property; in such instances the director shall at once consult the medical officer and report to the higher administrative authority.

34. The patterns and manner of use of instruments of restraint shall be decided by the central prison administration. Such instruments must not be applied for any longer time than is strictly necessary.

Information to and complaints by prisoners

35. (1) Every prisoner on admission shall be provided with written information about the regulations governing the treatment of prisoners of his category, the disciplinary requirements of the institution, the authorized methods of seeking information and making complaints, and all such other matters as are necessary to enable him to understand both his rights and his obligations and to adapt himself to the life of the institution.

(2) If a prisoner is illiterate, the aforesaid information shall be conveyed to him orally.

36. (1) Every prisoner shall have the opportunity each week day of making requests or complaints to the director of the institution or the officer authorized to represent him.

(2) It shall be possible to make requests or complaints to the inspector of prisons during his inspection. The prisoner shall have the opportunity to talk to the inspector or to any other inspecting officer without the director or other members of the staff being present.

(3) Every prisoner shall be allowed to make a request or complaint, without censorship as to substance but in proper form, to the central prison administration, the judicial authority or other proper authorities through approved channels.

(4) Unless it is evidently frivolous or groundless, every request or complaint shall be promptly dealt with and replied to without undue delay.

Contact with the outside world

37. Prisoners shall be allowed under necessary supervision to communicate with their family and

reputable friends at regular intervals, both by correspondence and by receiving visits.

38. (1) Prisoners who are foreign nationals shall be allowed reasonable facilities to communicate with the diplomatic and consular representatives of the State to which they belong. (2) Prisoners who are nationals of States without diplomatic or consular representation in the country and refugees or stateless persons shall be allowed similar facilities to communicate with the diplomatic representative of the State which takes charge of their interests or any national or international authority whose task it is to protect such persons.

39. Prisoners shall be kept informed regularly of the more important items of news by the reading of newspapers, periodicals or special institutional publications, by hearing wireless transmissions, by lectures or by any similar means as authorized or controlled by the administration.

Books

40. Every institution shall have a library for the use of all categories of prisoners, adequately stocked with both recreational and instructional books, and prisoners shall be encouraged to make full use of it.

Religion

41. (1) If the institution contains a sufficient number of prisoners of the same religion, a qualified representative of that religion shall be appointed or approved. If the number of prisoners justifies it and conditions permit, the arrangement should be on a full-time basis.

(2) A qualified representative appointed or approved under paragraph (1) shall be allowed to hold regular services and to pay pastoral visits in private to prisoners of his religion at proper times.

(3) Access to a qualified representative of any religion shall not be refused to any prisoner. On the other hand, if any prisoner should object to a visit of any religious representative, his attitude shall be fully respected.

42. So far as practicable, every prisoner shall be allowed to satisfy the needs of his religious life by attending the services provided in the institution and having in his possession the books of religious observance and instruction of his denomination.

Retention of prisoners' property

43. (1) All money, valuables, clothing and other effects belonging to a prisoner which under the regulations of the institution he is not allowed to retain shall on his admission to the institution be placed in safe custody. An inventory thereof shall be signed by the prisoner. Steps

shall be taken to keep them in good condition.

(2) On the release of the prisoner all such articles and money shall be returned to him except in so far as he has been authorized to spend money or send any such property out of the institution, or it has been found necessary on hygienic grounds to destroy any article of clothing. The prisoner shall sign a receipt for the articles and money returned to him.

(3) Any money or effects received for a prisoner from outside shall be treated in the same way.

(4) If a prisoner brings in any drugs or medicine, the medical officer shall decide what use shall be made of them.

Notification of death, illness, transfer, etc.

44. (1) Upon the death or serious illness of, or serious injury to a prisoner, or his removal to an institution for the treatment of mental affections, the director shall at once inform the spouse, if the prisoner is married, or the nearest relative and shall in any event inform any other person previously designated by the prisoner.

(2) A prisoner shall be informed at once of the death or serious illness of any near relative. In case of the critical illness of a near relative, the prisoner should be authorized, whenever circumstances allow, to go to his bedside either under escort or alone.

(3) Every prisoner shall have the right to inform at once his family of his imprisonment or his transfer to another institution.

Removal of prisoners

45. (1) When the prisoners are being removed to or from an institution, they shall be exposed to public view as little as possible, and proper safeguards shall be adopted to protect them from insult, curiosity and publicity in any form.

(2) The transport of prisoners in conveyances with inadequate ventilation or light, or in any way which would subject them to unnecessary physical hardship, shall be prohibited.

(3) The transport of prisoners shall be carried out at the expense of the administration and equal conditions shall obtain for all of them.

Institutional personnel

46. (1) The prison administration, shall provide for the careful selection of every grade of the personnel, since it is on their integrity, humanity, professional capacity and personal suitability for the work that the proper administration of the institutions depends.

(2) The prison administration shall constantly seek to awaken and

maintain in the minds both of the personnel and of the public the conviction that this work is a social service of great importance, and to this end all appropriate means of informing the public should be used.

(3) To secure the foregoing ends, personnel shall be appointed on a full-time basis as professional prison officers and have civil service status with security of tenure subject only to good conduct, efficiency and physical fitness. Salaries shall be adequate to attract and retain suitable men and women; employment benefits and conditions of service shall be favorable in view of the exacting nature of the work.

47. (1) The personnel shall possess an adequate standard of education and intelligence.

(2) Before entering on duty, the personnel shall be given a course of training in their general and specific duties and be required to pass theoretical and practical tests.

(3) After entering on duty and during their career, the personnel shall maintain and improve their knowledge and professional capacity by attending courses of in-service training to be organized at suitable intervals.

48. All members of the personnel shall at all times so conduct themselves and perform their duties as to influence the prisoners for good by their example and to command their respect.

49. (1) So far as possible, the personnel shall include a sufficient number of specialists such as psychiatrists, psychologists, social workers, teachers and trade instructors.

(2) The services of social workers, teachers and trade instructors shall be secured on a permanent basis, without thereby excluding part-time or voluntary workers.

50. (1) The director of an institution should be adequately qualified for his task by character, administrative ability, suitable training and experience.

(2) He shall devote his entire time to his official duties and shall not be appointed on a part-time basis.

(3) He shall reside on the premises of the institution or in its immediate vicinity. (4) When two or more institutions are under the authority of one director, he shall visit each of them at frequent intervals. A responsible resident official shall be in charge of each of these institutions.

51. (1) The director, his deputy, and the majority of the other personnel of the institution shall be able to speak the language of the greatest number of prisoners, or a language understood by the greatest number of them.

(2) Whenever necessary, the services of an interpreter shall be

used.

52. (1) In institutions which are large enough to require the services of one or more full-time medical officers, at least one of them shall reside on the premises of the institution or in its immediate vicinity.

(2) In other institutions the medical officer shall visit daily and shall reside near enough to be able to attend without delay in cases of urgency.

53. (1) In an institution for both men and women, the part of the institution set aside for women shall be under the authority of a responsible woman officer who shall have the custody of the keys of all that part of the institution.

(2) No male member of the staff shall enter the part of the institution set aside for women unless accompanied by a woman officer.

(3) Women prisoners shall be attended and supervised only by women officers. This does not, however, preclude male members of the staff, particularly doctors and teachers, from carrying out their professional duties in institutions or parts of institutions set aside for women.

54. (1) Officers of the institutions shall not, in their relations with the prisoners, use force except in self-defense or in cases of attempted escape, or active or passive physical resistance to an order based on law or regulations. Officers who have recourse to force must use no more than is strictly necessary and must report the incident immediately to the director of the institution.

(2) Prison officers shall be given special physical training to enable them to restrain aggressive prisoners.

(3) Except in special circumstances, staff performing duties which bring them into direct contact with prisoners should not be armed. Furthermore, staff should in no circumstances be provided with arms unless they have been trained in their use.

Inspection

55. There shall be a regular inspection of penal institutions and services by qualified and experienced inspectors appointed by a competent authority. Their task shall be in particular to ensure that these institutions are administered in accordance with existing laws and regulations and with a view to bringing about the objectives of penal and correctional services.

PART II: RULES APPLICABLE TO SPECIAL CATEGORIES

A. Prisoners under Sentence

Guiding principles

56. The guiding principles hereafter are intended to show the

spirit in which penal institutions should be administered and the purposes at which they should aim, in accordance with the declaration made under Preliminary Observation I of the present text.

57. Imprisonment and other measures which result in cutting off an offender from the outside world are afflictive by the very fact of taking from the person the right of self-determination by depriving him of his liberty. Therefore the prison system shall not, except as incidental to justifiable segregation or the maintenance of discipline, aggravate the suffering inherent in such a situation.

58. The purpose and justification of a sentence of imprisonment or a similar measure deprivative of liberty is ultimately to protect society against crime. This end can only be achieved if the period of imprisonment is used to ensure, so far as possible, that upon his return to society the offender is not only willing but able to lead a law-abiding and self-supporting life.

59. To this end, the institution should utilize all the remedial, educational, moral, spiritual and other forces and forms of assistance which are appropriate and available, and should seek to apply them according to the individual treatment needs of the prisoners.

60. (1) The regime of the institution should seek to minimize any differences between prison life and life at liberty which tend to lessen the responsibility of the prisoners or the respect due to their dignity as human beings.

(2) Before the completion of the sentence, it is desirable that the necessary steps be taken to ensure for the prisoner a gradual return to life in society. This aim may be achieved, depending on the case, by a pre-release regime organized in the same institution or in another appropriate institution, or by release on trial under some kind of supervision which must not be entrusted to the police but should be combined with effective social aid.

61. The treatment of prisoners should emphasize not their exclusion from the community, but their continuing part in it. Community agencies should, therefore, be enlisted wherever possible to assist the staff of the institution in the task of social rehabilitation of the prisoners. There should be in connection with every institution social workers charged with the duty of maintaining and improving all desirable relations of a prisoner with his family and with valuable social agencies. Steps should be taken to safeguard, to the maximum extent compatible with the law and the sentence, the rights relating to civil interests, social security rights and other social benefits of prisoners.

62. The medical services of the institution shall seek to detect and shall treat any physical or mental illnesses or defects which may hamper a prisoner's rehabilitation. All necessary medical, surgical and psychiatric services shall be provided to that end.

63. (1) The fulfilment of these principles requires individualization of treatment and for this purpose a flexible system of classifying prisoners in groups; it is therefore desirable that such groups should be distributed in separate institutions suitable for the treatment of each group.

(2) These institutions need not provide the same degree of security for every group. It is desirable to provide varying degrees of security according to the needs of different groups. Open institutions, by the very fact that they provide no physical security against escape but rely on the self-discipline of the inmates, provide the conditions most favorable to rehabilitation for carefully selected prisoners.

(3) It is desirable that the number of prisoners in closed institutions should not be so large that the individualization of treatment is hindered. In some countries it is considered that the population of such institutions should not exceed five hundred. In open institutions the population should be as small as possible.

(4) On the other hand, it is undesirable to maintain prisons which are so small that proper facilities cannot be provided.

64. The duty of society does not end with a prisoner's release. There should, therefore, be governmental or private agencies capable of lending the released prisoner efficient after-care directed towards the lessening of prejudice against him and towards his social rehabilitation.

Treatment

65. The treatment of persons sentenced to imprisonment or a similar measure shall have as its purpose, so far as the length of the sentence permits, to establish in them the will to lead law-abiding and self-supporting lives after their release and to fit them to do so. The treatment shall be such as will encourage their self-respect and develop their sense of responsibility.

66. (1) To these ends, all appropriate means shall be used, including religious care in the countries where this is possible, education, vocational guidance and training, social casework, employment counseling, physical development and strengthening of moral character, in accordance with the individual needs of each prisoner, taking account of his social

and criminal history, his physical and mental capacities and aptitudes, his personal temperament, the length of his sentence and his prospects after release.

(2) For every prisoner with a sentence of suitable length, the director shall receive, as soon as possible after his admission, full reports on all the matters referred to in the foregoing paragraph. Such reports shall always include a report by a medical officer, wherever possible qualified in psychiatry, on the physical and mental condition of the prisoner.

(3) The reports and other relevant documents shall be placed in an individual file. This file shall be kept up to date and classified in such a way that it can be consulted by the responsible personnel whenever the need arises.

Classification and individualization

67. The purposes of classification shall be:

(a) To separate from others those prisoners who, by reason of their criminal records or bad characters, are likely to exercise a bad influence;

(b) To divide the prisoners into classes in order to facilitate their treatment with a view to their social rehabilitation.

68. So far as possible separate institutions or separate sections of an institution shall be used for the treatment of the different classes of prisoners.

69. As soon as possible after admission and after a study of the personality of each prisoner with a sentence of suitable length, a programme of treatment shall be prepared for him in the light of the knowledge obtained about his individual needs, his capacities and dispositions.

Privileges

70. Systems of privileges appropriate for the different classes of prisoners and the different methods of treatment shall be established at every institution, in order to encourage good conduct, develop a sense of responsibility and secure the interest and co-operation of the prisoners in their treatment.

Work

71. (1) Prison labor must not be of an afflictive nature.

(2) All prisoners under sentence shall be required to work, subject to their physical and mental fitness as determined by the medical officer.

(3) Sufficient work of a useful nature shall be provided to keep prisoners actively employed for a normal working day.

(4) So far as possible the work provided shall be such as will maintain or increase the prisoners,

ability to earn an honest living after release.

(5) Vocational training in useful trades shall be provided for prisoners able to profit thereby and especially for young prisoners.

(6) Within the limits compatible with proper vocational selection and with the requirements of institutional administration and discipline, the prisoners shall be able to choose the type of work they wish to perform.

72. (1) The organization and methods of work in the institutions shall resemble as closely as possible those of similar work outside institutions, so as to prepare prisoners for the conditions of normal occupational life.

(2) The interests of the prisoners and of their vocational training, however, must not be subordinated to the purpose of making a financial profit from an industry in the institution.

73. (1) Preferably institutional industries and farms should be operated directly by the administration and not by private contractors.

(2) Where prisoners are employed in work not controlled by the administration, they shall always be under the supervision of the institution's personnel. Unless the work is for other departments of the government the full normal wages for such work shall be paid to the administration by the persons to whom the labor is supplied, account being taken of the output of the prisoners.

74. (1) The precautions laid down to protect the safety and health of free workmen shall be equally observed in institutions.

(2) Provision shall be made to indemnify prisoners against industrial injury, including occupational disease, on terms not less favorable than those extended by law to free workmen.

75. (1) The maximum daily and weekly working hours of the prisoners shall be fixed by law or by administrative regulation, taking into account local rules or custom in regard to the employment of free workmen.

(2) The hours so fixed shall leave one rest day a week and sufficient time for education and other activities required as part of the treatment and rehabilitation of the prisoners.

76. (1) There shall be a system of equitable remuneration of the work of prisoners.

(2) Under the system prisoners shall be allowed to spend at least a part of their earnings on approved articles for their own use and to send a part of their earnings to their family.

(3) The system should also provide that a part of the earnings should be set aside by the

administration so as to constitute a savings fund to be handed over to the prisoner on his release.

Education and recreation

77. (1) Provision shall be made for the further education of all prisoners capable of profiting thereby, including religious instruction in the countries where this is possible. The education of illiterates and young prisoners shall be compulsory and special attention shall be paid to it by the administration.

(2) So far as practicable, the education of prisoners shall be integrated with the educational system of the country so that after their release they may continue their education without difficulty.

78. Recreational and cultural activities shall be provided in all institutions for the benefit of the mental and physical health of prisoners.

Social relations and after-care

79. Special attention shall be paid to the maintenance and improvement of such relations between a prisoner and his family as are desirable in the best interests of both.

80. From the beginning of a prisoner's sentence consideration shall be given to his future after release and he shall be encouraged and assisted to maintain or establish such relations with persons or agencies outside the institution as may promote the best interests of his family and his own social rehabilitation.

81. (1) Services and agencies, governmental or otherwise, which assist released prisoners to re-establish themselves in society shall ensure, so far as is possible and necessary, that released prisoners be provided with appropriate documents and identification papers, have suitable homes and work to go to, are suitably and adequately clothed having regard to the climate and season, and have sufficient means to reach their destination and maintain themselves in the period immediately following their release.

(2) The approved representatives of such agencies shall have all necessary access to the institution and to prisoners and shall be taken into consultation as to the future of a prisoner from the beginning of his sentence.

(3) It is desirable that the activities of such agencies shall be centralized or coordinated as far as possible in order to secure the best use of their efforts.

B. Insane and Mentally Abnormal Prisoners

82. (1) Persons who are found to be insane shall not be detained in prisons and arrangements shall be

made to remove them to mental institutions as soon as possible.

(2) Prisoners who suffer from other mental diseases or abnormalities shall be observed and treated in specialized institutions under medical management.

(3) During their stay in a prison, such prisoners shall be placed under the special supervision of a medical officer.

(4) The medical or psychiatric service of the penal institutions shall provide for the psychiatric treatment of all other prisoners who are in need of such treatment.

83. It is desirable that steps should be taken, by arrangement with the appropriate agencies, to ensure if necessary the continuation of psychiatric treatment after release and the provision of social-psychiatric after-care.

C. Prisoners under Arrest or Awaiting Trial

84. (1) Persons arrested or imprisoned by reason of a criminal charge against them, who are detained either in police custody or in prison custody (jail) but have not yet been tried and sentenced, will be referred to as "untried prisoners,' hereinafter in these rules.

(2) Unconvicted prisoners are presumed to be innocent and shall be treated as such.

(3) Without prejudice to legal rules for the protection of individual liberty or prescribing the procedure to be observed in respect of untried prisoners, these prisoners shall benefit by a special regime which is described in the following rules in its essential requirements only.

85. (1) Untried prisoners shall be kept separate from convicted prisoners.

(2) Young untried prisoners shall be kept separate from adults and shall in principle be detained in separate institutions.

86. Untried prisoners shall sleep singly in separate rooms, with the reservation of different local custom in respect of the climate.

87. Within the limits compatible with the good order of the institution, untried prisoners may, if they so desire, have their food procured at their own expense from the outside, either through the administration or through their family or friends. Otherwise, the administration shall provide their food.

88. (1) An untried prisoner shall be allowed to wear his own clothing if it is clean and suitable.

(2) If he wears prison dress, it shall be different from that supplied to convicted prisoners.

89. An untried prisoner shall always be offered opportunity to work, but shall not be required to work. If he chooses to work, he shall be paid for it.

90. An untried prisoner shall be allowed to procure at his own expense or at the expense of a third party such books, newspapers, writing materials and other means of occupation as are compatible with the interests of the administration of justice and the security and good order of the institution.

91. An untried prisoner shall be allowed to be visited and treated by his own doctor or dentist if there is reasonable ground for his application and he is able to pay any expenses incurred.

92. An untried prisoner shall be allowed to inform immediately his family of his detention and shall be given all reasonable facilities for communicating with his family and friends, and for receiving visits from them, subject only to restrictions and supervision as are necessary in the interests of the administration of justice and of the security and good order of the institution.

93. For the purposes of his defense, an untried prisoner shall be allowed to apply for free legal aid where such aid is available, and to receive visits from his legal adviser with a view to his defense and to prepare and hand to him confidential instructions. For these purposes, he shall if he so desires be supplied with writing material. Interviews between the prisoner and his legal adviser may be within sight but not within the hearing of a police or institution official.

D. Civil Prisoners

94. In countries where the law perm its imprisonment for debt, or by order of a court under any other non-criminal process, persons so imprisoned shall not be subjected to any greater restriction or severity than is necessary to ensure safe custody and good order. Their treatment shall be not less favorable than that of untried prisoners, with the reservation, however, that they may possibly be required to work.

E. Persons Arrested or Detained Without Charge

95. Without prejudice to the provisions of article 9 of the International Covenant on Civil and Political Rights, persons arrested or imprisoned without charge shall be accorded the same protection as that accorded under part I and part II, section C. Relevant provisions of part II, section A, shall likewise be applicable where their application may be conducive to the benefit of this special group of persons in custody, provided that no measures shall be taken implying that re-education or rehabilitation is in any way appropriate to persons not convicted of any criminal offense.